MW00788890

Visual Antietam Vol. 1: Ezra Carman's Antietam Through Maps and Pictures: Dawn to Dunker Church

Ezra A. Carman

Edited and Illustrated by
Brad Butkovich

Copyright © 2018 Historic Imagination LLC

www.historicimagination.com

All rights reserved.

ISBN-13: 978-1-7325976-0-0

Dedication

This book is dedicated to my beautiful wife Holley, without whose patience and understanding this book, or any book of mine, would never see the light of day.

CONTENTS

Introduction

Ezra A. Carman looms large in the historiography of the Battle of Antietam. Colonel of the 13th New Jersey Infantry during the battle, he devoted a large portion of his later life to documenting the battle and preserving the battlefield. He "served as a trustee on the Antietam National Cemetery Association Board from 1866 to 1877 and as an 'historical expert' and member of the War Department's Antietam Board for Antietam National Battlefield Site from 1895 to 1897." He spent the better part of this period of his life writing a comprehensive manuscript detailing the Maryland Campaign, to include the battles at South Mountain before the battle, and the fight at Shepherdstown afterwards. In addition, he spent a significant amount of effort to build an accurate order of battle, along with the strength of the armies engaged. The result was a well-researched, and well written, account of the actions in Maryland and West Virginia during that fateful September. As part of his work, he created a series of maps showing the movement and flow of the battle over the course of the day. He even went so far as to revise them years after publication based upon the feedback and critique of fellow veterans. His work has served as the foundation for much of the subsequent writings on the battle. Though written more than a century ago, it holds up to modern scrutiny quite well. As historian Thomas G. Clemens wrote, "while a few inconsistencies and analytical judgments can be questioned, the remarkable point is how often Carman got it right."

I first became acquainted with the manuscript when it was included in the 1999 release of the computer game *Sid Meier's Antietam!*. I was fascinated by the detail presented in the document, but soon set it aside as I read other accounts, most notably John M. Priest's *Antietam: The Soldier's Battle* and Stephen W. Sears' *Landscape Turned Red: The Battle of Antietam*. However, it wasn't until farther along in the digital age, when I discovered and downloaded the Carman/Cope maps in high resolution from the Library of

Congress, that I was able to fully appreciate Carman's work.

My Civil War interests have always centered on maps and visual context. My website www.civilwarvirtualtours.com details several battles with maps, videos, and photos. For my previous battle studies on Pickett's Mill and Allatoona Pass I created all the maps myself. One day while discussing a new publication detailing the fight at the Cornfield at Antietam with friend and fellow author Scott Mingus Sr., he suggested I write my own book on the fight on that section of the battle. After giving it some thought, I wanted to make sure I incorporated many more maps than are usually presented in battle histories. Then I remembered Carman's manuscript. Instead of researching and writing my own text, I hit upon the idea of using Carman's text instead. In my opinion, it is still the most detailed and readable study of the battle currently available. Thus was born the idea for this three volume set.

The Visual Antietam series is intended for both readers who visit the battlefield, and those, perhaps overseas, who will never have the chance to see it. On every opposite page of the Carman text is an image to help the reader visualize the battlefield. The maps detail the movement the men and units far more often than most other works. There are pictures of the landscape, both period and modern, to help the reader understand the terrain and "lay of the land." And finally, where appropriate are pictures, not just of the generals, but also of the common soldiers and line officers that fought on the battlefield that day. Given the graphics heavy nature of the work, a single volume would have been too large. The series is divided into three volumes. Those wishing to visit the battlefield with the books and their maps can do so with individual volumes in a convenient carry size.

This series is not intended to be a detailed, heavily annotated study of the campaign or battle. The full, proper title of Carman's manuscript is *The Maryland Campaign of September 1862*. However, since I am focusing on only the battle itself, I have altered the title. Campaign chapters and those that do not relate directly to the battle have been omitted. There are few footnotes in the text. My purpose was to bring his book, and more specifically the battle, to life with an emphasis on visual context. For those wishing to read comprehensive versions of the Carman manuscript, digging into his source material and methods, I highly recommend Thomas Clemens' *The Maryland Campaign of September 1862. Volume II: Antietam* (and Volumes I and III of course) and Joseph Pierro's *The Maryland Campaign of September 1862: Ezra A. Carman's Definitive Study of the Union and Confederate Armies at Antietam*. Both are thoroughly researched and noted.

Very few editing changes were made to the manuscript. Some changes are for readability, some to bring the text up to modern standards. These include standardizing times by adding colons between the hour and minutes instead of periods, adding commas consistently to numbers between the thousands and hundreds, indenting large quotes, and changing book titles to italics. As stated, footnotes are minimal. I only used them to highlight important changes in the text, such as misspellings, as well as sections where Carman added large clippings from the *Official Records of the Rebellion*. Otherwise, Carman's idiosyncrasies have been left alone, such as using recrossed instead of re-crossed. Or Louisianians instead of Louisianans.

Volume 1

With the manuscript divided into three volumes, the first covers the crossing of Antietam Creek and the evening skirmish on September 16th, through the brutal action across the Miller farm the next morning. It concludes with the Union army finally expelling the Confederates from their positions in the Cornfield and East Woods, and their drive toward the West Woods and the Dunker Church. This is my favorite portion of the battle to study. This book is as much of a journey for me as it is for the reader. Creating the maps helped solidify my understanding of the flow of battle, more than any reading of existing texts. I hope readers will experience the same comprehension epiphany while reading the book and maps together.

Most of the pictures in this work were taken as close as possible to the hour they occurred in 1862, even taking modern daylights savings time into account. As such, some of them show sharp contrast and shadows. For example, when looking east into the sun, the East Woods appears darker. This is more apparent in Volume 1 than others, given that the battle began before dawn. While it may have been more prudent to take the photos in better light, this is how the soldiers viewed the landscape around them during the battle.

Carman's manuscript is a wide ranging work spanning the Maryland Campaign, the battles for the South Mountain passes, and the actions afterwards around Shepherdstown. The Battle of Antietam itself, naturally, falls in the middle. This is why the first chapter of this work is titled Chapter 13 instead of Chapter 1.

Visual Antietam Vol. 2: Ezra Carman's Antietam Through Maps and Pictures: The West Woods To Bloody Lane will continue the narrative as the Union press their advantage in the West Woods, and turn south to confront the Sunken Road or Bloody Lane. *Visual Antietam Vol. 3: Ezra Carman's Antietam Through Maps and Pictures: The Middle Bridge To Hill's Counterattack* concludes the manuscript with the fighting around the Middle and Burnside's Bridge crossings of the Antietam, and Ambrose P. Hill's counterattack.

Acknowledgments

This book would not have been possible without the help and assistance from several people. As noted, Scott Mingus gave me the idea that led to the development of this series in the first place. He has also graciously written the Foreword, and has always been available for advice and ideas since I first started writing.

Scott Felsen, when he's not hiking the Pickett's Mill battlefield, agreed to accompany me on the long drive to the Antietam National Battlefield Park and share his photography expertise. He was a great help with framing and lighting advice, and we were able to take more than enough images for all three volumes.

I also wish to thank my proofreaders Andy Papen, Patrick McCormick, and Scott Felsen for reading over the manuscript and pointing out all those little details and layout errors that escape the eye when you've stared at the same words for months at a time. Their help was invaluable.

Finally, I'd like to thank my wife Holley and my kids, for tolerating me writing on Saturdays and sometimes being away on trips to Civil War battlefields.

Foreword

Antietam is today best remembered as "America's Bloodiest Day," with almost 23,000 casualties (with most occurring in only half a day). The pitched battle on September 17, 1862, near Sharpsburg, Maryland, was in some ways a massive chess match between Confederate General Robert E. Lee and his often-cautious Union adversary, Maj. Gen. George B. McClellan. The latter, having superior numbers of almost two-to-one, largely wasted his massive advantage in manpower by launching a series of mostly uncoordinated attacks involving individual corps with minimal effective-range artillery support. This gave the aggressive Lee the time to quickly shift troops and artillery pieces to counter McClellan's moves and to patch holes in the thinly-stretched, beleaguered Confederate line. In some measures, this was perhaps Lee's finest job of professional generalship, keeping his understrength forces from breaking under the various Union attacks while awaiting the arrival of reinforcements then rushing up from Harper's Ferry.

Lee had established his defensive lines behind Antietam Creek after good work by several subordinates at the battles on South Mountain on September 14. Major General D. H. Hill and others had held three entire Union corps at bay in the narrow mountain passes to buy enough time for Lee to concentrate as much as his scattered Army of Northern Virginia as he could. Now, on the 17th, with A. P. Hill's "Light Division" of the army still at Harper's Ferry, Lee and his trusted senior lieutenants, James Longstreet and Thomas "Stonewall" Jackson, managed to parry every one of McClellan's piecemeal assaults, though at great cost to both contending armies. Fighting did not resume on the following day and Lee was able to slip back into Virginia after a rear-guard action at the Potomac River crossing at Shepherdstown. McClellan did not aggressively pursue the Rebels, a miscalculation that greatly aggravated President Lincoln and officials of the U. S. Department of War and eventually led to McClellan's dismissal as commander of the Army of the Potomac.

Today, the scenic rolling fields of the Antietam National Battlefield are quiet and serene, dotted with scores of impressive stone and metal monuments recalling the long-ago valor of American soldiers, both those wearing blue and those wearing the butternut and gray. Visitors to the neatly kempt National Cemetery can reverently pay their respects to those men who "gave their last full measure of devotion" during the battle. Others carefully study the battlefield in person, noting how the terrain and creek greatly influenced the combat action. Some eagerly follow the exploits of a particular general, or a regiment or battery of personal interest. For some visitors, it the tactics and weaponry that are of most interest, or perhaps the human element of the more than 100,000 combatants, many of whom left personal accounts of their actions during the battle and the Maryland Campaign as a whole. Often, the visitors use the services of a professional guide to assist them in understanding the fighting and its impact, leading to Lincoln writing the Emancipation Proclamation.

Among those soldiers who left accounts of their experiences at Antietam was Ezra Ayers Carman, who spent much of his lifetime corresponding with other veterans of the battle and capturing their recollections. Born in New Jersey and educated at the Western Military Institute, he served as the lieutenant colonel of the 7th New Jersey early in the war before being wounded in his arm at the battle of Williamsburg in May 1862. Returning to action late that summer as colonel of the freshly-recruited 13th New Jersey, he fought at Antietam along the Hagerstown Pike and near the Dunker Church. He ended the war as a brigadier general. Carman was later a key member of the Antietam Battlefield Board, which oversaw the preservation of the hallowed grounds.

Antietam remains a battle worthy of study. While there have been dozens of good books written over the past century about the combat, there is still plenty of room for additional scholarship. However, Carman's lengthy manuscript, drawn from his own memory and augmented greatly by his extensive communication with other veterans, is often considered as the starting point for many researchers and battlefield buffs.

Brad Butkovich, a long-time miniature wargamer and historical researcher, has combined his talents for mapmaking and editing in this new rendition of Carman's classic account of the fighting at Sharpsburg, its prelude, and its aftermath. This engrossing work is a fine addition to his earlier book on the May 1864 battle of Pickett's Mill in northern Georgia and to his wargaming scenario books on Antietam and other battles with their beautifully drawn, accurate maps. Butkovich's fine maps have effectively captured the strategic and tactical elements of the Maryland Campaign and they collectively present a clear and concise treatment of the various segments of the fighting near Antietam Creek. Carman's prose, in

Brad's capable hands as editor, make this volume and its planned successors a worthwhile addition to any Civil War book collection.

Scott L. Mingus, Sr.
York, Pennsylvania
Author of *Human Interest Stories from Antietam*

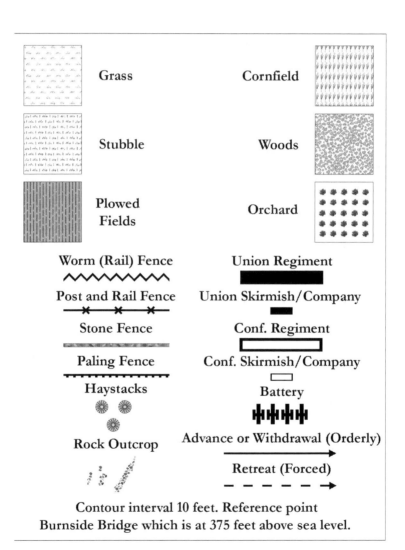

Grass

Cornfield

Stubble

Woods

Plowed Fields

Orchard

Worm (Rail) Fence

Union Regiment

Post and Rail Fence

Union Skirmish/Company

Stone Fence

Conf. Regiment

Paling Fence

Conf. Skirmish/Company

Haystacks

Battery

Rock Outcrop

Advance or Withdrawal (Orderly)

Retreat (Forced)

Contour interval 10 feet. Reference point
Burnside Bridge which is at 375 feet above sea level.

Chapter 13

The Prelude to Antietam (September 16, 1862)

General Lee was an early riser. On the night of the 15th his headquarters were pitched in a body of open woods nearly three-fourths of a mile west of the Sharpsburg town square, on the right of the road leading to Shepherdstown. Very soon after daybreak of the 16th he had breakfast and was on Cemetery Hill, and after walking among the guns of the Washington Artillery, trying in vain to pierce the fog that hung over the course of the Antietam, to see what McClellan was doing, walked back to the roadside, where a campfire was smoldering. Here, about sunrise, a young officer of Longstreet's staff rode up, dismounted, and delivered a message, to which Lee listened attentively, then as in a soliloquy, said: "All will be right if McLaws gets out of Pleasant Valley." Still earlier in the morning he had heard that the head of Jackson's column had reached the Potomac and that, when Jackson left Harper's Ferry, McLaws was still in the valley, but had been ordered by Jackson to follow him as soon as possible.

We return to Jackson and Walker, whom we left at Harper's Ferry and Loudoun Heights on the morning of the 15th. We have noted the receipt by Jackson of Lee's orders to join him as speedily as possible, but Jackson's men were out of rations and these could not be immediately supplied. Late in the afternoon General A. R. Lawton, commanding Ewell's division, was ordered to march to Sharpsburg, 14 miles distant. Two only of his brigades—Lawton's and Trimble's—were ready and Lawton started with these near sunset, leaving General Early, with his brigade and Hays', to follow as soon as possible. Lawton marched up the Virginia side of the Potomac until late in the night and went into camp about four miles from Shepherdstown Ford. Early was not promptly supplied with rations, and it was midnight when they had been cooked. At 1 a.m. he marched with his brigade and Hays' and overtaking Lawton, the entire division was on the march at early dawn, crossed Shepherdstown Ford at sunrise and, proceeding on the Sharpsburg road, halted in a wood, about a mile from town, near Jackson's Division, that had preceded it in crossing the Potomac.

No sooner had the surrender of Harper's Ferry been assured than Walker descended Loudoun Heights, crossed the Shenandoah at Keys' Ferry and marched to Halltown, where he halted for rations. At 1 a.m. he resumed his march, overtook the rear of Jackson's force, about an hour later, and reached Shepherdstown Ford between daylight and sunrise. His division crossed the river early in the day, and halted in a grove about midway from the ford to Sharpsburg, where it remained until 3 a.m. of the 17th, when it moved to the right and took position to cover Snavely's and Myers' fords south of Sharpsburg.

Jackson made this report:

> Leaving Hill to receive the surrender of the Federal Troops and take the requisite steps for securing the captured stores, I moved, in obedience to orders from the commanding general, to rejoin him in Maryland with the remaining divisions of my command. By a severe night march we reached the vicinity of Sharpsburg on the morning of the 16th.

Some of Jackson's staff officers and others say that Jackson reported to Lee at daylight on Cemetery Hill. General Walker says that he rode forward with Jackson from Shepherdstown Ford about 8 o'clock. In another article in the volume referred to he says that after the troops had crossed the Potomac he rode forward with Jackson at midday to report to Lee:

> I expected to find General Lee anxious and careworn. Anxious enough, no doubt he was; but there was nothing in his look or manner to indicate it. On the contrary, he was calm, dignified, and even cheerful. If he had a well organized army of 100,000 veterans at his back, he could not have appeared more composed and confident. On shaking hands with us, he simply expressed his satisfaction with the result of our operation at Harper's Ferry, and with our timely arrival at Sharpsburg; adding that with our reinforcements he felt confident of being able to hold his ground until the arrival of the divisions of R. H.

Major General Thomas J. Jackson
Library of Congress

Anderson, McLaws and A. P. Hill, which were still behind, and which did not arrive until the next day. Jackson and Walker brought to Lee about 10,300 officers and men. This was not a large reinforcement but, with 15,600 already in position, gave Lee an aggregate of infantry, cavalry, and artillery of 25,900 men, all veteran soldiers. It was a compact, well trained force. As the long September day wore on, and gave the men time to rest, Lee became confident that he would not be called upon for any serious work that day and, that by morning, McLaws and Anderson would be with him, his army, except for A. P. Hill reunited and ready to give McClellan battle.

During the afternoon and night of the 15th McClellan's forces moved to the positions assigned them, but it was not until after daybreak of the 16th that the great body of them were in their designated places, some brigades did not get up until noon. Hooker's (First) Corps was in the forks of the Big and Little Antietam. Sumner's (Second) Corps was on both sides of the Boonsboro and Sharpsburg road, Richardson's Division in advance, near the Antietam, on the right of the road. Sykes' Division was on the left of Richardson's, and on Sykes' left and rear was Burnside's (Ninth) Corps. Mansfield's (Twelfth) Corps was at Nicodemus Mill or Springvale. Pleasonton's cavalry division was just west of Keedysville.

Near midnight of the 15th two companies each of the 61st and 64th New York, under command of Lieutenant Colonel Nelson A. Miles, passed along the rear of Sedgwick's Division and some distance along the bluff below the "middle bridge," then turning back reached the bridge just as a party of Union cavalry came riding sharply over it from the south bank. They informed Miles that the enemy had fallen back and that there were none in the immediate front of the bridge. Miles crossed the bridge to the west side of the creek, and marched cautiously west along the highway. It was then daybreak. A heavy fog prevented vision for more than fifteen or twenty feet; the dust in the road deadened the sound of the footsteps and silence was enjoined. Miles who was in advance, had reached the crest of the ridge about 600 yards beyond the Antietam, and was about to descend into the broad ravine where the Confederates were in position, when he ran upon a Confederate crossing the road, whom he captured and from whom he learned, that he was very near the Confederate line. The command was faced about and moved back with as much silence as possible, and recrossed the bridge before the fog lifted, but long after daylight of the 16th.

There has been much criticism on the failure of McClellan to attack Lee on the afternoon of the 15th or at least early on the 16th. We have referred to the failure to do so on the 15th. The situation, inviting prompt attack on

Lieutenant Colonel (later Major General) Nelson A. Miles
Library of Congress

the morning of the 16th, is well stated by General F. A. Walker in the *History of the Second Army Corps*:

> If it be admitted to have been impracticable to throw the thirty-five brigades that had crossed the South Mountain at Turner's Gap across the Antietam during the 15th, in season and in condition to undertake attack upon Lee's fourteen brigades that day with success, it is difficult to see what excuse can be offered for the failure to fight the impending battle on the 16th, and that early. It is true that Lee's forces had then been increased by the arrival of Jackson with J. R. Jones and Lawton's divisions (also Walker's), but those of Anderson, McLaws and A. P. Hill could not be brought up that day. A preemptory recall of Franklin, in the early evening of the 15th, would have placed his three divisions in any part of the line that might be desired. Even without Franklin, the advantages of concentration would have been on the side of McClellan. When both armies were assembled the Union forces were at least nine to six, of the Confederate six only four could possibly have been present on the 16th. Without Franklin the odds would still have been seven to four.

It is evident that McClellan had no idea of fighting Lee on the 15th. There seems to have been no intention to do it early on the 16th, certainly no orders to that effect were issued, nor did he make any preparations. In fact he expected Lee to retreat during the night of the 15th.

At 9 o'clock on the morning of the 16th, after telegraphing his wife that he had no doubt "delivered Pennsylvania and Maryland," McClellan dispatched Halleck:

> The enemy yesterday held a position just in front of Sharpsburg. This morning a heavy fog has thus far prevented us doing more than to ascertain that some of the enemy are still there. Do not know in what force. Will attack as soon as situation of enemy is developed.

When the fog lifted he missed S. D. Lee's guns, which had been moved to the left, or, as he reports:

> It was discovered that the enemy had changed the position of his batteries. The masses of his troops, however, were still concealed behind the opposite heights. Their left and center were upon and in front of the Sharpsburg and Hagerstown Turnpike, hidden by woods and irregularities of the ground, their extreme left resting upon a wooded eminence near the cross-roads to the north of Miller's farm, their left resting upon the Potomac (sic in McClellan's report). Their

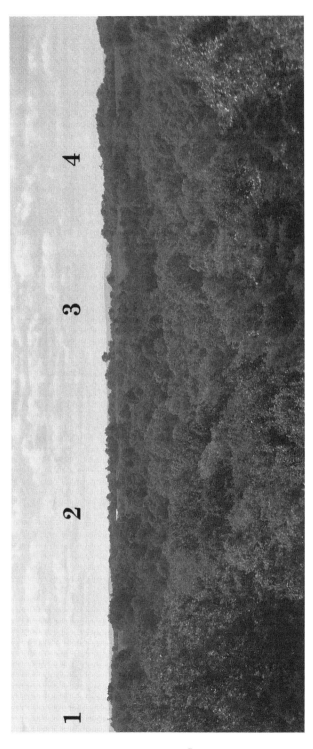

Looking west across the battlefield from the Pry House and McClellan's headquarters. In 1862 the intervening trees were not present. Visible landmarks are: (1) The New York monument, site of Colonel Stephen D. Lee's artillery battalion. (2) The roof of the Mumma barn. (3) The open fields south of the Cornfield, and the Cornfield itself. (4) The East Woods. *Scott Felsen.*

line extended south, the right resting upon the hills to the south of Sharpsburg near Snavely's farm.

The changed position of the batteries is given by McClellan as one of the reasons for not making the attack before afternoon, for, he says, he was "compelled to spend the morning in reconnoitering the new position taken up by the enemy, examining the ground, finding fords, clearing the approaches, and hurrying up the ammunition and supply trains, which had been delayed by the rapid march of the troops over the few practicable approaches from Frederick. These had been crowded by the masses of infantry, cavalry and artillery pressing on with the hope of overtaking the enemy before he could form to resist an attack. Many of the troops were out of rations on the previous day, and a good deal of their ammunition had been expended in the severe action of the 14th.

From the time of McClellan's arrival on the field until Hooker's advance in the afternoon of the 16th, nothing seems to have been done with a view to an accurate determination of the Confederate position. From the heights east of the Antietam the eye could trace the right and center, but the extreme left could not be definitely located, nor was the character of the country on that flank known. It was upon this flank that McClellan decided to make his attack and one would suppose that his first efforts would be directed to ascertain how that flank could be approached and what it looked like. This was proper work for cavalry, of which he had a good body available for the purpose. Pleasonton's cavalry division was in good shape and elated with its successful achievements, culminating in the discomfiture of Fitz-Hugh Lee's Brigade at Boonsboro, the day before, and confident of its capacity for further good work. But it was not used. As far as we know not a Union cavalryman crossed the Antietam until Hooker went over in the afternoon of the 16th, when the 3rd Pennsylvania cavalry accompanied him. Nor can we discover that the cavalry did any productive work elsewhere. It did not ascertain that there were good fords below the Burnside Bridge, leading directly to the right-rear of the Confederate line, and we know of no order given for its use, save a suggestion to Franklin, to have his cavalry feel towards Frederick. The part taken by the cavalry this day is very briefly told by Pleasonton, in his report: "On the 16th my cavalry was engaged in reconnaissances, escorts and support to batteries." If any part of his command, except the 3rd Pennsylvania, was engaged in reconnaissances and supporting batteries we do not know of it.

The first movement of the day was to crown the bluff east of the Antietam with artillery and cover the Middle Bridge. This bluff, which, south of the bridge, almost over-hangs the Antietam, recedes from it north of the bridge for a short distance, then approaches it. It rises 180 feet above the stream and commands nearly the entire battlefield.

Monroe A. White, Company D, 11th United States Infantry
Library of Congress

The Reserve Artillery, which arrived late in the evening of the 15th, was put in position, early in the morning, by General Henry J. Hunt, chief of artillery. Taft's New York battery, and the German (New York) batteries of von Kleiser, Langner, and Wever were placed on the bluff north of the Boonsboro road, Taft's Battery relieving Tidball's which rejoined the cavalry division. Von Kleiser relieved Pettit's New York battery. The four New York batteries had 20 pound Parrott guns and were supported by Richardson's Division. South of the Boonsboro road, and about 9 a.m. Weed's Battery (I, 5th U.S.) and Benjamin's Battery (E, 2nd U.S.) were run up the bluff in front of Sykes' Division. Each battery, as it came into position, opened upon such bodies of Confederate infantry as could be seen, and upon the Washington Artillery and Hood's Division batteries, on Cemetery Hill, and the batteries on the ridge running north from it, and the reply was prompt and spirited, during which Major Albert Arndt, commanding the German artillery battalion, was mortally wounded.

As the Confederates were short of ammunition and the range too short for their guns, Longstreet ordered them to withdraw under cover of the hill. General D. H. Hill says that the Confederate artillery was badly handled and "could not cope with the superior weight, calibre, range, and number of the Yankee guns. An artillery duel between the Washington Artillery and the Yankee batteries across the Antietam, on the 16th, was the most melancholy farce in the war."

At 1 p.m. Taft's and von Kleiser's batteries were moved from the north to the south of the Boonsboro road; Taft relieving Benjamin, who went to the left, near Burnside Bridge, and von Kleiser taking position about 120 yards on Weed's right. Kusserow's Battery, of 20-pound Parrotts[1], relieved Taft, north of the road, but not in the same position. From Taft's, von Kleiser's, and Weed's positions one could look to the right, through the open space between the East and West Woods, and see Hood's men as they advanced to meet Hooker, late in the day, and their guns were brought to bear upon them, as also, upon Jackson's men as they took position near the Dunker Church, about sunset. From the bluff north of the Boonsboro road the gunners could look down the Sunken road, and it appeared but a stone's throw to Piper's cornfield in and around which were the men of Rodes' Brigade. There were very few points of the Confederate line that these batteries could not reach, and on many they had an enfilade and reverse fire.

---

[1] Kusserow's Battery D, 1st Battalion New York Artillery actually consisted of six 32-pdr. Howitzers. Curt Johnson and Richard C. Anderson Jr. *Artillery Hell: The Employment of Artillery at Antietam* (College Station: Texas A&M University Press, 1995), p. 23.

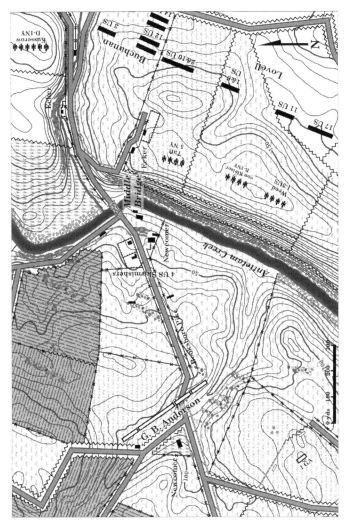

Late afternoon positions on Sept. 16th around the Middle Bridge. Approximate positions after the arrival of the 1st Georgia Regulars but before the 12th United States relieved the 4th United States at the Bridge.

Early in the morning a signal station was established on the crest of Elk Ridge. The extensive view from this position commanded Sharpsburg and Shepherdstown, the country in the vicinity, and the approaches in every direction. It communicated with signal stations at McClellan's headquarters, with some on the extreme right, and with Burnside's headquarters.

Sykes' Division was on the south side of the Boonsboro road, its right, Buchanan's Brigade, resting on the road, opposite Richardson's left. On the left of Buchanan was Lovell's Brigade, extending down toward the Burnside Bridge. Warren's Brigade of two New York regiments (5th and 10th) were held in reserve. Later in the day, it, with Randol's Battery (E and G, 1st U.S.) was moved to the left, out of the line of fire of the Confederate guns on Cemetery Hill; the new position in a piece of woods, and covering the approaches in the direction of Harper's Ferry. At 7 a.m. Captain Hiram Dryer, 4th U.S. Infantry, was ordered to take the Middle Bridge and establish part of his regiment on the west bank of the Antietam.

Upon arriving within 200 yards of the bridge he passed the pickets of the 3rd U.S. Infantry, when he detached Lieutenant John L. Buell, Company G, to advance rapidly to the bridge, which was done without opposition. Dryer then marched the regiment to the bridge and threw four companies across it, which were posted under cover of a stone bank and wall on the right of the road, and of a rock-ledge and barn on the left. In about two hours it was observed that the enemy was advancing a skirmish line on both sides of the road, upon which, two companies, under Lieutenant Buell and R. P. McKibbin, advanced on either side of the road to hold the Confederate in check. They advanced about 300 yards up the ascending road and met the enemy, who, after exchanging a few shots, fell back under cover of the ridge, behind which lay George B. Anderson's Brigade. About the same time the Confederate batteries on Cemetery Hill began a vigorous shelling of Dryer's skirmishers and upon the batteries on the bluff in his rear, beyond the Antietam. The firing was of short duration and did but little harm, wounding 3 of Dryer's men, two others were wounded by the skirmishers. At sunset Dryer was relieved by the 1st Battalion, 12th U.S. Infantry, Captain M. M. Blunt, and recrossed the Antietam. As soon as the bridge had been taken by the regular infantry, two companies of the 5th New Hampshire, under Captains Cross and Long were sent to destroy the mill-dam a few yards below the bridge, hoping thus to lower the waters of the creek above and make fording less difficult, but did not succeed in breaking the dam, for want of proper tools. Several companies of Richardson's division were on picket during the night, and in the morning, four companies of the 5th New Hampshire, under Major E. E. Sturtivant, were detached to guard a small aqueduct, crossing the Antietam near Neikirk's, nearly a mile above the bridge.

Picture of the embankment north of the Middle Bridge and Boonsboro Turnpike where companies of the 4th United States Infantry took shelter. *Author's collection.*

During the forenoon the Twelfth Corps advanced from its bivouac near Nicodemus' Mill and massed in a field west of Keedysville and in rear of French's Division. In the afternoon, Morell's Division of the Fifth Corps passed through Keedysville and bivouacked on the left of the Boonsboro and Sharpsburg Turnpike.

The valley of the Antietam at and near the Burnside Bridge is narrow. On the right of the stream the high bank was wooded below the bridge and about 200 yards above it, and commanded the approaches both to the bridge and the ford immediately below it. The steep slopes of the bank were lined with rifle pits and breastworks of rails and stones. These, together with the woods, were filled with Toombs infantry, while numerous batteries commanded and enfiladed the bridge and ford and their approaches.

McClellan seems to have had some apprehension that the Confederates might attack his left by this bridge and by the valley below it and, about noon, ordered Burnside to move farther to the left, to a strong position in the immediate vicinity of the bridge and to reconnoiter the approaches to it carefully, as he would probably be ordered to attack there on the next morning. Later in the day he rode to the left to satisfy himself that Burnside had properly placed his troops to secure his left flank from any attack made along the east bank of the Antietam, as well as to carry the bridge. He was not satisfied with the dispositions made by Burnside and found it necessary to order some changes, the result of which was that, late in the afternoon, Burnside's Corps, except Willcox's Division, was moved to the left and front, in three columns, and took position upon the rear slopes of the ridge on the east bank of the Antietam, the center of the corps being nearly opposite the bridge, the batteries were placed on the crest of the hill near the bridge, the infantry in close support, Benjamin's Battery being on a knoll, some distance to the left and back from the bridge.

Burnside's movement was not opposed, nor disturbed, save by a few shots from Richardson's Battery, south of Cemetery Hill, but Toombs' skirmish line thrown across the bridge for observation, was seen, near a cornfield southeast of the bridge, upon which Captain H. F. Duval, with his company of the 36th Ohio, went forward and drove it through the cornfield and back over the bridge. About the same time Capt. James Wren with a detachment of the 48th Pennsylvania went a mile down the Antietam and saw nothing but Munford's cavalry, on the west bank of the stream.

The 79th New York was detached and sent to guard the signal station at McClellan's Gap on Elk Ridge, and the 28th Massachusetts and 50th Pennsylvania, both under command of Major Edward Overton, were sent to Elk Ridge, where the Rohrersville road crossed it, to support some of Pleasonton's cavalry, which was keeping open the communications with Franklin in Pleasant Valley.

Major General Ambrose E. Burnside.
Library of Congress.

General McClellan reports that the ground in front of the entire Confederate line consisted of undulating hills, their crests, in turn commanded by others in their rear.

> On all favorable points the enemy's artillery was posted, and their reserves, hidden from view by the hills on which their line of battle was formed, could maneuver unobserved by our army, and, from the shortness of their line, could rapidly re-enforce any point threatened by our attack. This position, stretching across the angle formed by the Potomac and the Antietam, their flanks and rear protected by these streams, was one of the strongest to be found in this region of country which is well adopted to defensive warfare.

When McClellan made his rapid examination on the evening of the 15th, he concluded that an attack on the Confederate left offered better results than an attack elsewhere, and the conclusion was confirmed by a more extended examination on the morning of the 16th. For reasons given elsewhere, which we consider entirely inadequate, he deferred the movement until afternoon.

The plan for the impending general engagement was to attack Lee's left with the corps of Hooker and Mansfield, supported by Sumner's corps and, if necessary, by Franklin's corps, and, as soon as matters looked favorably there, to move Burnside's corps, against Lee's right, upon the ridge running to the south and rear of Sharpsburg. Having carried these positions he then proposed to press with the right along the crest towards Sharpsburg, and when either of these flank movements should be successful to advance the center across the Middle Bridge with all the forces then disposable. The plan was a good one, but its execution, from beginning to end was miserable, though the fighting was splendid.

The first step in McClellan's plan was the transfer of Hooker's First Corps to the west bank of the Antietam. If this movement was not itself a reconnaissance in force, it should have been preceded by such an examination of the ground as would have sufficed to determine, with some approach to accuracy where Lee's left was, but this, as we have seen, was not done. The first step was a blunder, in that the movement was made in the afternoon of the 16th, at an hour too late to accomplish anything before dark and serving no purpose, save to inform Lee where he was to be attacked.

It was 2 p.m. when McClellan gave Hooker orders to cross the Antietam by the Upper Bridge and ford below it, to attack and, if possible, turn Lee's left; Meade's and Ricketts' division were to cross the bridge and Doubleday's at the ford. Later, Sumner was ordered to cross the Twelfth Corps during the night and hold the Second Corps in readiness to cross

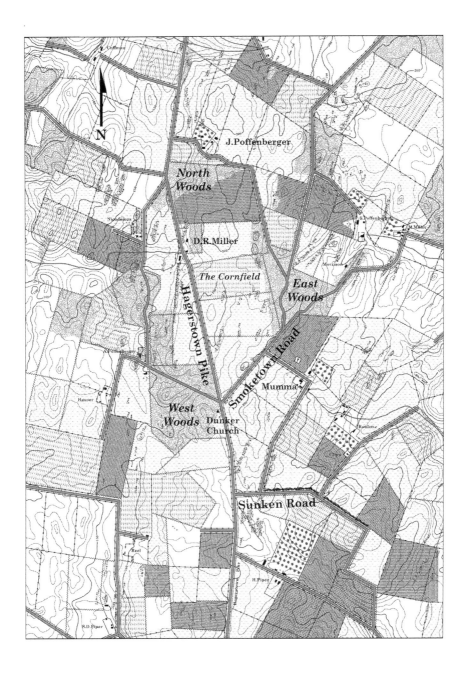

early next morning. It was nearly 4 p.m. when Hooker put his troops in motion, Meade's Division in advance. Then he rode to McClellan's headquarters for any further orders he might have to give, and was informed by McClellan that he was at liberty to call for reinforcements, should he need them, and, that on their arrival they would be placed under his command, upon which he rode off and joined his troops on the march. His direction lay nearly perpendicular to the Antietam, his object being to gain the high ground or divide between the Antietam and the Potomac, and then incline to the left, following the elevation towards Sharpsburg, feeling for Lee's flank, which it was believed would be found somewhere on the divide, its exact or even approximate position being unknown to either McClellan or Hooker that day or early on the next.

Meade's Division led the advance across the bridge and on the Williamsport road, two regiments being thrown forward as skirmishers, followed by a squadron of Lieut. Col. Samuel W. Owen's 3rd Pennsylvania Cavalry, all closely supported by the division. Hooker, as was his custom, rode in advance close to the skirmishers, and had not proceeded over half a mile when he was joined by McClellan and his staff, apparently to see how Hooker was progressing. "Among other subjects of conversation," reports Hooker, "I said to the general that he had ordered my small corps, now numbering between 12,000 and 13,000 (as I had just lost 1,000 men in the battle of South Mountain) across the river to attack the whole rebel army, and that if reinforcements were not forwarded promptly, or if another attack was not made on the enemy's right, the rebels would eat me up." Soon after this conversation McClellan recrossed the Antietam and rode to the Pry house from which he could see across the Antietam and observe the effect of Hooker's march or any movement made to meet it. From this time Pry's house became his headquarters. Ricketts' Division followed Meade's over the bridge and on the Williamsport road, and most of the artillery and all of the ammunition trains followed Ricketts.

Doubleday's Division crossed at Pry's Ford, below the bridge, drove some Confederate cavalrymen from a cornfield and strip of woods on the left, who hastened to inform Stuart, at the Dunker Church, that the Union army was crossing the upper Antietam, Stuart, in turn, sending the information to Lee at Sharpsburg. Doubleday first moved up stream a short distance, then, turning to the left, advanced over fields, parallel with Ricketts, and about 80 yards on his left, his entire division was closed up, Patrick's Brigade in the advance, removing fences and filling their pockets and haversacks with apples from the numerous, well laden orchards.

While Hooker's columns are in motion, we return to General Lee, whom we left congratulating Jackson and Walker upon the successful operations at Harper's Ferry and their timely arrival at Sharpsburg. It was with great satisfaction that he contemplated McClellan's delay in attacking his position,

William B. Todd, Company A, 9th Virginia Cavalry.
Library of Congress.

a delay he did not take advantage of to strengthen his position by the construction of any defenses. The utility of hastily constructed intrenchments on the field was not yet appreciated. But the delay gave him an opportunity to make a thorough study of the field, to select and occupy the best defensive positions, to give Jackson's and Walker's men a good rest, and concentrate more closely his widely separated command.

During the afternoon Lee, Longstreet, and Jackson held council in the house of Jacob A. Grove, at the southwest corner of the Sharpsburg town square. While they were examining the map of Maryland and a map of Washington County, the artillery on Cemetery Hill opened fire, word came that there was a movement threatening Burnside Bridge and a cavalryman dashed up with a message from Stuart that the Union forces were crossing the Antietam near Pry's Mill.

Lee at once ordered Longstreet to meet this advance on the left with Hood's Division, and Jackson was ordered to take position with his own division on Hood's left, Lawton's Division being ordered to support Toombs at the Burnside Bridge. Walker remained in reserve, near Lee's headquarters, west of town.

Early in the day the greater part of Fitz-Hugh Lee's cavalry brigade was in the fields near the Dunker Church, with detachments in advance on the Hagerstown road and on the Smoketown road and east of it, observing the crossings of the Antietam. The 9th Virginia, which had spent a quiet night in an oak grove near Sharpsburg, moved up the Hagerstown road during the day, passed Hood's men, at and in front of the Dunker Church, went down the Smoketown road beyond the East Woods and drew up in rear of two guns of Pelham's Battery, near the northwest corner of the S. Poffenberger woods. The guns were masked by a clump of bushes. The position commanded an extended view of open fields and the road leading to Smoketown, thence to the Antietam.

When the videttes came in and reported that the Union columns were crossing the Antietam by the bridge and the ford, dispositions were made to delay their march, and Stuart and Hood, who were at the Dunker Church, were notified. Stuart prepared Fitz-Hugh Lee's Brigade to support the 9th Virginia, should it be hard pressed, and Hood sent a company of the 2nd Mississippi, under R. E. Clayton, and one of the 6th North Carolina, under Captain Lea, up the Hagerstown road to D. R. Miller's. About 100 men of the 4th Texas, under command of Captain W. R. Martin, went northeast from the church, through the 30 acre cornfield, and grass field beyond, and took position on the right of the two companies of Clayton and Lea, and behind the fence overlooking the field between it and the North Woods, as also the ground on the right and the Smoketown road, beyond the East Woods. Other skirmishers of Hood's Division and some dismounted cavalry were behind the north fence of the East Woods and, on the right of

20

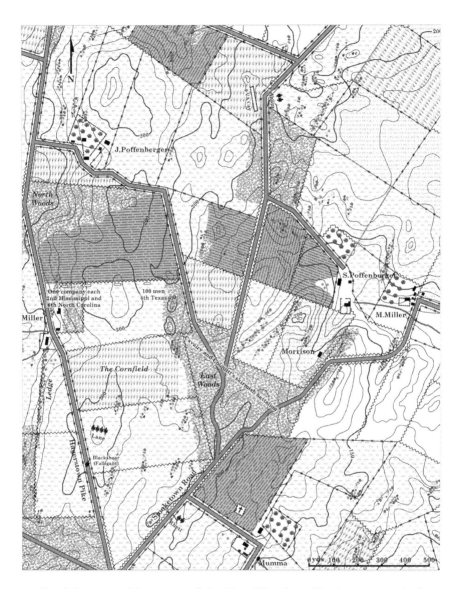

Confederate positions around the East Woods as Hooker approached.
The location of the 9th Virginia, Colquitt's battalion, and Pelham are
approximate.

those of the 4th Texas; and still farther to the right was a skirmish battalion of Colquitt's Brigade. Colonel S. D. Lee sent two howitzers of Rhett's South Carolina battery, to the left of the Mumma house, and quite near the Smoketown road, and a section of Parker's Virginia battery, went up the Hagerstown road, nearly a mile to the toll-gate, soon returning without becoming engaged. D. H. Hill sent Lane's Battery of Cutts' Battalion to assist Hood, and it took position between the Smoketown and Hagerstown roads. Hood says he stationed "one or two batteries upon a hillock in a meadow near the edge of a cornfield and just by the pike." One of them was Lane's Battery, the other we cannot identify, but it was what Wofford reports as "a little battery." On the Hagerstown road and about 180 yards south of the southwest corner of the cornfield, was one gun of Blackshear's Georgia battery under charge of Sergeant-Major R. Falligant. Later in the day, about sunset, three guns of Poague's Virginia battery, went into position on the left of Falligant, and about 40 yards west of the Hagerstown road.

When the advance of Meade's Division had gone less than a mile, Hooker saw at a distance the high ground he was seeking, upon which Meade's column turned to the left, off the road and across the Hoffman farm. Meanwhile detachments of the 3rd Pennsylvania Cavalry had been sent forward on the Williamsport road, also due west to locate the Hagerstown road, some of the latter went down the Smoketown road and were fired on by cavalry and artillery. The presence of the enemy was reported to Hooker just as he was leaving the road to march across the Hoffman farm, upon which he ordered the "Bucktails" (13th Pennsylvania Reserves) of Seymour's Brigade, to advance as skirmishers, on the left, and four companies of the 3rd Pennsylvania Reserves to deploy to the right; the main column, formed of battalions in mass, division front, with the artillery, moving the open ground, for the high ridge. Meanwhile a squadron of the 3rd Pennsylvania Cavalry, under Lieut. E. W. Warren, moving to the left and by the farm lane running past M. Miller's, had reached the south corner of the East Woods, where it was soon joined by a platoon of cavalry, under Lieut. W. E. Miller, which had advanced down the Smoketown road, followed by the "Bucktails," upon which Warren charged into the woods, unmasked the Confederate guns and was fired on by Virginia cavalry. Feeling that his instructions to develop the enemy had been carried out, Miller and Warren fell back and awaited the infantry now coming up.

Colonel Hugh W. McNeil, commanding the "Bucktails" had deployed four companies as skirmishers, the remaining six being held in reserve, and advancing steadily and cautiously, on either side of the Smoketown road, came upon the Confederate cavalry pickets in front of the East Woods, supported by troops in position behind the fence on the north edge of the woods. A body of Confederate cavalry dashed out of the woods and up the

The 13th Pennsylvania Reserve's view down the Smoketown Road from the southern edge of the Samuel Poffenberger woods. The trees on the right side of the road and left background were not present in 1862. The East Woods would have been visible in the background. *Author's collection.*

Smoketown road, over the Bucktail skirmishers, but were quickly driven back. The Confederate infantry skirmishers were driven in, and the "Bucktails," advancing, came under a raking fire from the infantry and dismounted cavalry, behind the fences, which was replied to, the reserve of six companies moving at once to the support of the skirmishers. No sooner had line been formed, in a plowed field, back of some hay-stacks, when the Confederates opened on it with two batteries, Rhett's with shell and Lane's with solid shot and spherical case.

Up to this time Hood's Division had remained near the Dunker Church, supporting the batteries which were firing beyond the East Woods, but when, at twilight, the cavalry was driven in, Hood went to the front to contest possession of the East Woods and the cornfield. Wofford's Brigade, which was in the field in front of the church, moved by the left flank and formed line on the south border of the cornfield, its left near the Hagerstown road, its right, the 5th Texas, in the East Woods. Law's Brigade moved from the woods about the church, directly to the front, the left wing on the left of the Smoketown road, supporting Wofford, the right wing on the right of the road and facing the eastern part of the East Woods. Scarcely had the division taken position when the cavalry and Pelham's two guns came back through the East Woods, passed through the deployed line of the division and went to the rear. The 5th Texas then sent forward a skirmish company through the cornfield, over the fence, and across a narrow pasture to a rail fence overlooking a plowed field, and saw Hooker's men advancing—Seymour's Brigade, with the "Bucktails" leading.

Col. McNeil, after forming line in the plowed field west of S. Poffenberger's, four companies on the right of the Smoketown road and six on the left, rested some fifteen minutes, during which time the remainder of the brigade came up, when he gave the order to charge and drive the enemy from the woods. Placing himself at the front, and, on the left of the road, he led his command, under a severe fire of the Texans and artillery, to within 15 yards of the East Woods, when he fell pierced to the heart by a rifle ball. The regiment did not pause but kept on, drove the enemy from the fence and entered the woods, to be checked when half-way through them by the 5th Texas and a battery on the south edge of Miller's cornfield. With the assistance of Cooper's and Ransom's guns the battery was soon silenced, but the Texans held ground. In this movement the "Bucktails" were closely supported by the remainder of the brigade, the 6th Reserves, advancing on their right, driving in the skirmishers of the 4th Texas and some of the 5th Texas, and slowly following them into the woods and to the fence separating the woods from the Miller cornfield. An effort was made to penetrate the cornfield but the right of Wofford's Brigade had pushed up into it and held ground so tenaciously that the regiment withdrew about 100 yards to the north part of the East Woods, leaving a

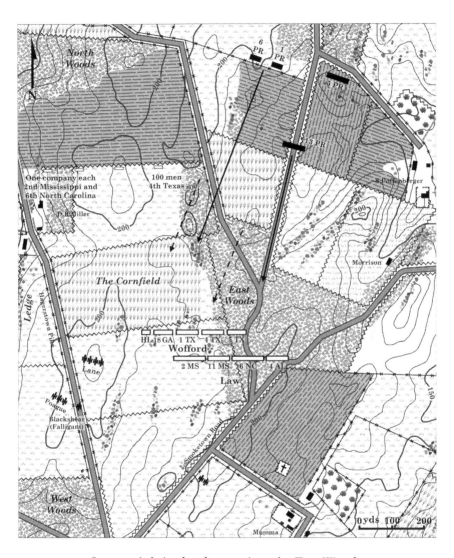

Seymour's brigade advances into the East Woods.

heavy picket line along the fence in its front. The 1st Reserves followed the "Bucktails" into the woods and formed on their right and rear. The 5th Reserves, on the left of the brigade, remained some time in the open ground, but came up after dark and formed along the north fence of the woods, on the left of the 1st Reserves.

Cooper's Pennsylvania Battery closely followed the "Bucktails" through the woods south of Line's, by a wagon path, down the Smoketown road, and into battery west of the road, close to the northwest corner of the S. Poffenberger woods, the 2nd Reserves in support, and opened fired upon Lane's Georgia Battery, which was firing at Seymour's men in the East Woods. While in this position and actively at work, the two brigades of Magilton and Anderson were swinging to the left and advancing past the right of the battery.

When the "Bucktails" moved down the Smoketown road to meet the enemy in that direction, Meade led the brigades of Magilton and Anderson toward the high ground and the Hagerstown road, but soon after leaving the Line farm and crossing the Smoketown road, when he had reached the crest of a gentle slope, he wheeled to the left and marched south, the column closed in mass, with skirmishers well out, stopping occasionally to remove fences and make observations. When nearing the J. Poffenberger barn the enemy's skirmishers were discovered in the North Woods and a battery beyond the woods and quite near the Hagerstown road opened fire, upon which four companies of the 3rd Pennsylvania Reserves were deployed as skirmishers to the right and four companies directly to the front, followed by the 4th Reserves in line of battle, closely supported by the two brigades. The Confederate skirmishers were quickly driven from the woods and the two brigades pushed on and occupied them just at dusk, Anderson's right resting on the Hagerstown road, with Magilton on his left.

When approaching the North Woods a Confederate battery was plainly seen in a field, beyond them, supported by infantry, playing upon Seymour's men in the East Woods. Major John Nyce ordered the 4th Pennsylvania Reserves to fix bayonets and prepared to take it, but was restrained by the order of his brigade commander, probably so directed by Meade, who says that as but one regiment, the 4th Reserves, was deployed he was deterred from the endeavor to capture the battery by a charge. After Meade entered the woods, the battery still continuing to fire on Seymour, Ransom's Battery (C, 5th U.S.) was ordered forward to silence it. Ransom went straight down the field east of the J. Poffenberger barn, through the North Woods to the open field beyond and into battery, opening upon the Confederate battery and supporting infantry an enfilade fire, which, in addition to Cooper's fire, and the musketry fire of the "Bucktail" skirmishers, caused the withdrawal of the offending guns. Wofford reports he had one officer and some dozen men wounded by this fire and that the enemy were informed of his position

Looking south from the edge of the North Woods in the evening. Ransom's Battery C, 5th United States deployed in this area during the fight at dusk on the 16th. *Author's collection.*

by the firing of a half dozen shots from a little battery on the left of his brigade which hastily beat a retreat as soon as the Union guns opened on it. About this time Poague's Battery of three guns, west of the Hagerstown road, began shelling Ransom's guns and the North Woods, occupied by Meade's men, and the hill beyond them. After a few shots at Poague's Battery, in which it was joined by Simpson's Pennsylvania Battery, Ransom was withdrawn and bivouacked a few yards north of the North Woods and east of J. Poffenberger's barn. Cooper remained in the position occupied at the beginning of the action and Simpson remained on the ridge a little to the right and rear of Cooper.

The losses in this affair were not heavy. On the Union side the principal loss fell upon the "Bucktails" in the death of their commander. Of Hood's Division but three regiments and the divisional skirmishers were engaged, these lost very lightly, and the left of Wofford's Brigade suffered some from artillery fire. Colonel P. E. Liddle, 11th Mississippi, was mortally wounded. His regiment was in the south edge of the cornfield, supporting Wofford's Brigade, and was not engaged, when he was struck by a chance shot.

While Hood was engaged, Jackson came on the field with his old division and formed on his left. When he received Lee's orders to take this position, he advanced from where he had been resting since morning, leaving Sharpsburg to the right, passed the Dunker Church and formed partly in open ground, and partly in woods, with his right on the Hagerstown road opposite Hood's left, Winder's' and Jones' brigades in front, on open ground, Taliaferro and Starke in the edge of the woods, a short distance in rear. Poague's Battery was on a slight knoll in advance of the first line, and, as we have seen, became engaged with Ransom's Battery, concerning which Poague says: "upon this battery, fire was opened, and in about twenty minutes it was silenced, our own battery (Lane's) on the right of the road in the meantime having retired. In this affair we were assisted by one gun of some unknown battery." This one gun, unknown to Poague, was Sergeant Falligant's gun of Blackshear's Battery. General J. R. Jones, commanding Jackson's Division, reports that the skirmishers were "warmly engaged until night" and Major H. J. Williams, of Winder's Brigade, says of the Union artillery fire, "the display was grand and comparatively harmless, except to the stragglers in far rear." But the second line suffered some casualties. Colonel Edmund Pendleton, 15th Louisiana, who succeeded to command of Starke's Brigade, next day, reports that in taking position, "we encountered the shells from three of the enemy's batteries (Cooper, Ransom, and Simpson), and had the misfortune about dark to have several of our number, among whom was the gallant young Gordon, a lieutenant in the 9th Louisiana Regiment and acting assistant adjutant-general of the brigade, who was killed by a shell which cut off both his legs at the thigh."

From the position of General John R. Jones' (Jackson's) Division looking north along the west side of the Hagerstown Turnpike. This first line would initially be held by Grigsby's and Jones' Brigades. *Author's collection.*

At the time Jackson's Division was sent to the left, Lawton was ordered to support Toombs at the Burnside Bridge. It was soon seen that no serious work was to be looked for in that quarter upon which Lawton was ordered to follow Jackson. He moved through the fields to west and north of Sharpsburg, until he reached the Hagerstown road at the Dunker Church. It was then growing dark, the troops in front were engaged, and Early's Brigade was formed on the left of Jackson's second line, and at right angles to it., to protect that flank. Hays' Brigade was put in Early's rear, Lawton's and Trimble's were held in reserve near the church.

About the time Jackson came up, Stuart's cavalry fell to the rear of Hood's Division, and, for a time rested in the fields east of the church and observed the shells from two directions, passing over head, "their burning fuses, making fiery streaks and gleaming like meteors, and the whole making a comparatively harmless but brilliant spectacular performance."

Of Hooker's Corps, Meade's Division only was engaged. The movement of this column to the left, slowly followed by Ricketts, interfered with the march of Doubleday's Division. When Meade, moving south, had passed the head of Doubleday's column, Patrick's Brigade was double-quicked west, under a sharp artillery fire, by which some men were wounded, to a triangular piece of woods skirting the Hagerstown road, and formed line along the road fence, facing west. Before the other brigades of the division could be put in motion to follow Patrick, Ricketts' Division crossed their line of march and moved into the S. Poffenberger woods, on either side of the Smoketown road, and bivouacked. After Ricketts had passed, the other three brigades of Doubleday resumed march in the dark. Hoffman's [Hofmann][2] Brigade halting on Patrick's left, and close to the fence of the road, his left connecting with Meade's right, at a right angle, and resting within a few feet of a lane running from the Hagerstown road to J. Poffenberger's. Phelps' small brigade followed Hofmann and bivouacked 200 yards in rear of Patrick. Gibbon's Brigade, closed in mass, bivouacked in rear of Hofmann. All of Doubleday's brigades faced west and were then at right angles to Meade, who faced south.

North of the Joseph Poffenberger house is a prominent hill or rounded ridge 220 feet above the Antietam, and the highest point of the battlefield, dominating all the ground west of the Hagerstown road and destined to play an important part in the battle of the 17th. It was on the western slope of this ridge that Doubleday's four brigades went into bivouac, and on its plateau were placed the division batteries. Campbell's Battery (B, 4th U.S.) was about 70 yards north of the Poffenberger barn; Monroe's (D, 1st Rhode Island) on Campbell's right, and Reynolds (L, 1st New York) on the

---

[2] Carman misspells his name as Hoffman. The correct spelling is Hofmann, as evidenced by his signed reports in the *Official Records*.

The Joseph Poffenberger house and barn. Photograph taken in the 1930s. *Library of Congress.*

right of Monroe. The 1st New Hampshire Battery, Lieutenant F. M. Edgell, went into park, in a cornfield, about 500 yards east of the ridge, where it remained until 3:30 a.m. of the 17th, when it advanced into position between Patrick's and Hofmann's brigades, close to the Hagerstown road, one gun on the road prepared to be used in any direction.

Hooker's movement was barren of good results but prolific in bad ones. When darkness came and stopped his advance, he knew very little more of the enemy's position than when he crossed the Antietam. He had been ordered to turn Lee's left flank, and completed his day's work by posting his own command in such manner as to secure it from a flank attack of the enemy, a very proper thing to do, under all circumstances, but a thing not contemplated when he started; he had given Lee complete and reliable information as to McClellan's intentions for the morrow.

Pickets were thrown out to the front and on the right, who were very close to those of the enemy, and, in the fore part of the night, the Confederate artillery kept up an annoying fire, particularly upon the brigades of Magilton and Anderson in the North Woods.

About 9 p.m. Colonel Fisher of the 5th Pennsylvania Reserves, on the left of the line, having some apprehension for that flank, sent Lieutenant H. P. Petriken with a detail of 24 men to reconnoiter and establish a picket post to the left and about 180 yards to the front. After passing the northeast corner of the East Woods, Petriken turned to the right and moved over a field east of the woods. It was so dark that objects were scarcely discernible at the distance of only a few feet, and as the party neared a fence running easterly from the southeast corner of the woods, smoldering campfires were seen and some of the men cautioned Petriken that the enemy were just behind the fence. Petriken ordered his party forward and, when about 25 feet from the fence, the 4th Alabama and part of the 6th North Carolina, of Law's Brigade, fired a scattering volley. The detachment gave a partial volley in return and retreated, leaving Petriken mortally wounded. He was taken by the Alabama men to the Dunker Church and tenderly cared for, but died during the night. His watch was returned to his family by Capt. W. M. Robbins of the 4th Alabama.

At his headquarters in the Poffenberger barn Hooker heard the picket firing along the line in his immediate front, and still farther to the left on Seymour's front and, soon after the Petriken incident, visited his pickets in order to satisfy himself concerning this firing. He found that the picket lines were so near each other that though unseen, each could hear the other walk. Seymour's officers and men were keenly alive to their propensity to the enemy and appeared to realize the responsible character of their service for the night. Their conduct inspired Hooker with the fullest confidence. Upon returning to the barn, Hooker immediately dispatched a courtier informing McClellan of his surroundings and assuring him that the battle would be

Major General Joseph Hooker (photographed while Brigadier General)
Library of Congress.

renewed at the earliest dawn and that reinforcements should be ordered forward in season to reach him before that moment.

The 3rd Pennsylvania Cavalry, after performing much detached duty during the day, was practically united soon after dark, between the right of Seymour's Brigade and the left of Magilton. Late in the night, a squadron, under command of Captain Claude White, was ordered on outpost duty. When giving White his instructions, Hooker said he could not give any information about the roads, that he had taken position on the left flank of the enemy and wanted him to move to the right and rear and use his eyes and ears so as to give him timely notice of any movement in that quarter on the part of the enemy. White moved north, more than a mile from Hooker's headquarters, to the intersection of the Williamsport road and the Hagerstown turnpike, placing his reserves in the angle of the two roads, at the Schneibele home and picketing the turnpike and the road west of it.

When the engagement terminated by darkness, Stuart moved his cavalry still farther to the left, on Jackson's flank, and crowned the commanding hill between the West Woods and the Potomac with artillery ready for the attack in the morning. The greater part of Fitz-Hugh Lee's Brigade was moved in rear of this steep hill and near the river. It was quite late in the night when Fitz- Hugh Lee got into position, after which he went up the side of the hill, tied his horse to a small tree and lay down to sleep. Jackson soon came up and laid down near him at the foot of a tree and was soon asleep.

The 7th Virginia Cavalry, of Munford's Brigade, was detached September 10th, to accompany Jackson on his march to Harper's Ferry. On the afternoon of the 16th it recrossed the Potomac at Shepherdstown Ford and marched by Grove's, Smith's and Rowe's to the Coffman farm, where the horses were left and the men marched across the fields to Ground Squirrel Church, and took position north of the woods, which surround the church, and on both sides of the Hagerstown turnpike. It was late at night and they were not aware of the fact that they were but 600 yards south of White's squadron of the 3rd Pennsylvania Cavalry and but half a mile north of Doubleday's Division. Nor did the Pennsylvania cavalrymen nor Doubleday's men know of the near presence of the Virginians.

When it became evident to General Lee that Hooker's movement was but the advance of a much larger force and that his left was to be attacked early in the morning, he ordered D. H. Hill to extend his line to the left, which Hill did by moving Ripley's Brigade from the right, near the Boonsboro and Sharpsburg turnpikes, to the left and in support to Jackson and Hood and the batteries of Stephen D. Lee. Ripley passed in the rear of the division and took position, during the night, about 150 yards west of the Mumma house, his right resting on Mumma's lane, his left extending northwest nearly to the Smoketown road.

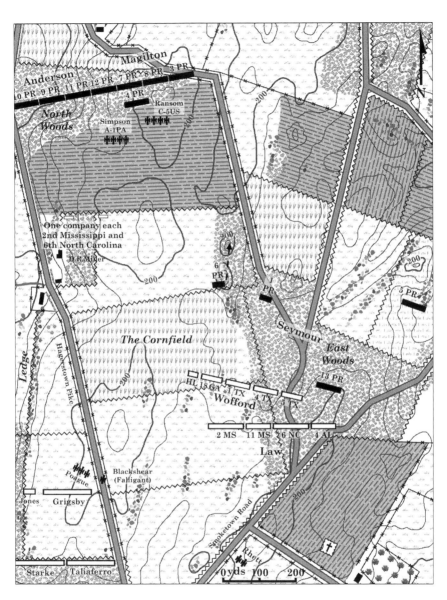

Approximate positions around the East Woods at nightfall September 16th.

The officers and men of Hood's Division, being without food for three days, except a half ration of beef for one day, and green corn gathered from the field, Hood rode back to Lee's headquarters and requested him to send two or more brigades to his relief, or at least for the night, in order that his men might have a chance to cook their meager rations of flour. Lee said that he would cheerfully do so, but he knew of no command that could be spared for the purpose; he, however, suggested that Hood see Jackson and endeavor to obtain assistance from him. After riding a long time in search of Jackson, Hood finally found him alone, lying on the ground, asleep, by the foot of a tree. He aroused him and made known the half-starved condition of his troops, upon which Jackson ordered Lawton's and Trimble's brigades to his relief. He exacted of Hood, however, a promise that he would move to the support of these brigades the moment he was called upon. It was now after 10 o'clock, his two brigades were relieved and fell back to a position about 200 yards in rear of the Dunker Church and Hood rode off in search of his wagons, that his men might prepare to cook their flour.

Lawton's Brigade relieved the Texas Brigade; two companies of skirmishers, under Lieutenant W. H. Harrison, 31st Georgia, about 50 feet in the south edge of Miller's cornfield, extending into the East Woods on the right and to the Hagerstown pike on the left; eight companies of the 31st Georgia, in support, about 100 yards south of the corn, the remainder of the brigade, in line, about 135 yards behind the 31st Georgia. Trimble's Brigade, commanded by Colonel James A. Walker, 13th Virginia, relieved Law: its pickets in the edge of the East Woods, which were occupied but a short distance farther in by Seymour's men, and his main line in a plowed field, east of the Smoketown road, one regiment in a clover field west of the road and connecting, though not closely, with Lawton on the left. The right connected with Ripley's Brigade, the latter forming nearly a right angle with Walker, and fronting the Antietam. Lawton faced north; Walker northeast. Both brigades lay upon their arms during the night with occasional skirmishing in front between the pickets.

There is nothing in the records to show that, when Hooker crossed the Antietam, it was the intention of McClellan that either the Twelfth or Second Corps should follow him that evening, if there were such intentions they were not shown in any orders to that end. But when McClellan, after his march with Hooker, recrossed the Antietam he ordered Sumner to send the Twelfth Corps to Hooker's support that evening and to hold his own, Second Corps, in readiness to march for the same purpose an hour before daylight. Sumner, who was anxious to have his command of two corps act as a unit, under his own eye, in so far as this was possible, asked permission to follow Mansfield's Corps that night, but McClellan would not consent;

Brigadier General Alexander R. Lawton. His division would play an important part in the struggle for the Cornfield early in the morning on the 17th. *Library of Congress.*

he would give him no authority to move till ordered to do so, and was given to understand that he would not receive such orders till next morning. McClellan had broken up Burnside's wing command by detaching Hooker, he now dislocated Sumner's by detaching Mansfield.

Sumner sent the order to Mansfield late in the night and the corps, crossing the Little Antietam and main Antietam by the stone bridges, went up the Williamsport road nearly a mile, then turned to the left and, about 2:30 a.m., went into bivouac on the farms of Hoffman and Line, a mile in Hooker's rear. Sumner, anticipating the movement of his own corps, and impressed with the importance of having everything at the front at the very earliest hour, sent five of his batteries across the Antietam during the night. They parked near the Twelfth Corps.

Chapter 15

The Battle on the Union Right and the Confederate Left (Daybreak to 7:30 a.m.)

The battle of Antietam (or Sharpsburg) was really three distinct engagements, at different hours of the day, on entirely different parts of the field. The battle began on the Union right at daybreak and was practically over at 10:30 a.m. In the center it began at 9:30 a.m. and was over before 1 p.m. It began on the Union left at 10 a.m. and continued until sunset. No Union troops that fought on one part of the line were elsewhere engaged. With the Confederates it was different: Colonel Walter H. Taylor, in *Four Years with General Lee*, says "With consummate skill were they maneuvered and shifted from point to point, as different parts of the line of battle were in turn assailed with greatest impetuosity."

The engagement on the right began with the advance of the First Corps, under Hooker, at daybreak, upon the divisions of Ewell and Jackson, resulting in the defeat of those two divisions and the check of Hood's Division. The next stage was the advance of the Twelfth Corps and its relief of the First Corps at 7:30 a.m.; the forcing back Hood and successful engagement with the brigades of Ripley, Colquitt, and Garland, driving them from the field at 8:40 a.m. The third stage, on the right, was the advance of the Second Corps at 9:10 a.m., and, the engagement of Sedgwick's Division and parts of the First and Twelfth corps, in the West Woods, with Early's and G. T. Anderson's brigades, the divisions of McLaws and Walker, and the remnants of Jackson's Division.

39

When Hooker crossed the Antietam, on the afternoon of the 16th, it was his understanding that, when he began the attack the next morning, on Lee's left, simultaneous attacks would be made upon Lee's center and right. When he had taken position at night he reported to McClellan that "the battle would be renewed at the earliest dawn," and suggested that he should be reinforced before that time.

There was no delay on Hooker's part. The stars were still shining when his skirmishers became engaged and he and Meade left their quarters in the Poffenberger barn and went to the south edge of the North Woods to give direction to the attack. His examination determined him to continue a southward movement and seize what appeared to be the key point on that part of the field—the Dunker Church and the high ground adjacent, on either side of the Hagerstown road. Once gained, this position would take D. H. Hill's Division in left flank and rear, and enfilade the Confederate batteries on Cemetery Hill. Orders were given holding Doubleday's Division in readiness to move directly on the church and for batteries to be put in position to support the movement and silence Colonel S. D. Lee's guns, plainly seen on the plateau across the road from the church. While these examinations were being made the battle opened in the East Woods, between Seymour's men and the Confederate brigades of Lawton and Trimble, and by an artillery duel between Doubleday's batteries on the Poffenberger Hill and three batteries on Nicodemus hill. Ricketts was ordered to support Seymour; Doubleday's was ordered forward, and Meade's Division was held in the center to support the movement of Doubleday and Ricketts and go to the assistance of either, when required.

The Confederate position was not exactly as Hooker expected to find it. It did not present its flank to him; the left was thrown back at nearly a right angle to the main Confederate line, with its left across the Hagerstown road; Jackson's old division west of and perpendicular to the road, and two brigades of Ewell's Division, under A. R. Lawton, east of it. Lawton claims first attention.

Trimble's Brigade, under command of Colonel James A. Walker, 13th Virginia, was on the right of the division, its right resting on the Mumma grave-yard, thence extending to the left across the Smoketown road. From right to left were the 15th Alabama, 21st North Carolina, 21st Georgia, 12th Georgia, the last named being on the left of the road. The brigade numbered about 700 men. Ripley's Brigade of D. H. Hill's Division was on the right and rear of Trimble's. On the left of Trimble's was Lawton's Brigade, but not in close connection, there being an interval of 65 to 70 yards. Lawton's Brigade, commanded by Colonel Marcellus Douglass, 13th Georgia, had six Georgia regiments—the 13th, 26th, 31st, 38th, 60th, and 61st—numbering 1,150 men. When first in position, and until the battle had fairly opened, the left of the brigade was about 120 yards east of the

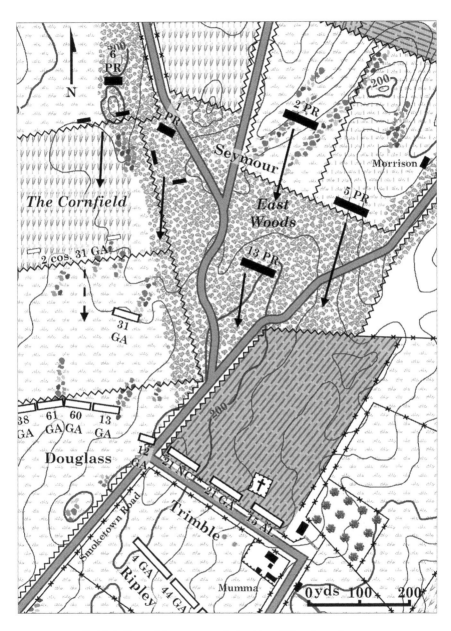

Initial dispositions around the East Woods at dawn.

Hagerstown road, and the three left regiments—the 26th, 38th, and 61st, in order named from left to right— from 225 to 230 yards south of the Miller cornfield and practically parallel to it; the right wing of the brigade was refused and faced northeast. The 31st Georgia was thrown to the front and left of the right wing, and to within 120 yards of the cornfield, its right about 100 yards from the East Woods fence. When taking position, during the night of the 16th, two companies of the 31st, under command of Lieutenant W. H. Harrison, were advanced as pickets 50 feet into the corn, their right at the edge of the East Woods, their left extending to the Hagerstown road. Before daybreak of the 17th Harrison inadvertently stumbled upon the Union picket line, a few shots were fired, Harrison was captured, and his pickets were withdrawn from the corn and formed along its south border. The ground held by the brigade was somewhat lower than the cornfield, and, in nearly its entire length, was covered by low stone ledges, and small protuberances, which afforded some protection and, in places, a rail fence was thrown down and piled as a breastwork. In other places there was no protection, either of rock-ledge, inequality of the ground, or fence rails, but as the action progressed and the line rapidly thinned, those exposed positions were abandoned for the sheltered ones.

In rear of Lawton's two brigades, on the plateau nearly opposite and about 225 yards from the church, were four batteries of Colonel S. D. Lee's artillery battalion—the Ashland (Va.) Artillery, Captain P. Woolfolk, Jr.; Bedford (Va.) Artillery, Captain T. C. Jordan; Brooks' (S. C.) Artillery, Lieutenant William Elliot; and Parker's (Va.) Battery, Captain W. W. Parker.

There was also in the vicinity of the church and on the ridge south and west of it some guns of Cutts' artillery battalion. The battalion consisted of the four Georgia batteries of Lane, Ross, Patterson, and Blackshear. Lane's Battery was not engaged on the 17th. The other three batteries were engaged on various parts of the field, in the vicinity of the church and on Hauser's ridge, most of the time under direction of General Stuart.

There was some spiteful firing during the night by the opposing pickets, who, in places, were not over 50 feet apart and, when not yet fairly dawn, the firing increased to the proportions of a severe engagement. Seymour's men soon advanced through the eastern part of the Miller's cornfield and the East Woods to the fences bordering them on the west, drove in the right of the skirmish line and fell upon the front and right flank of the eight companies of the 31st Georgia, who were driven back upon their brigade.

The 13th Pennsylvania Reserves (Bucktails) now advanced in somewhat open order about 100 yards to the left and front, still keeping in the woods and throwing its right forward, the left in this movement reaching and resting on the Smoketown road. In this position, well covered by the large trees, it opened a steady and very accurate fire upon both Trimble's Brigade and the right of Lawton's, while the skirmish lines of the 1st and 6th

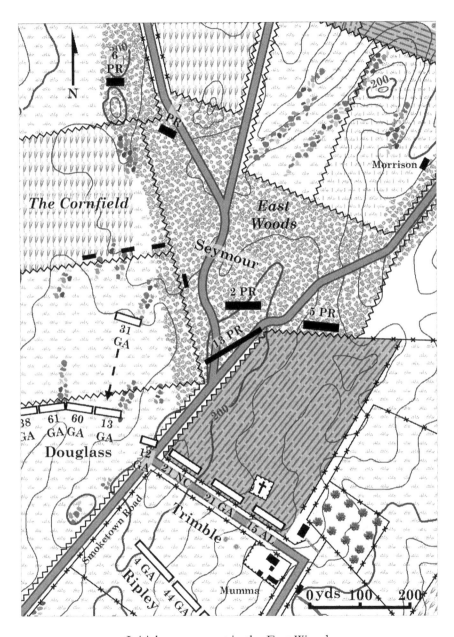

Initial engagement in the East Woods

Reserves advanced to the edge of the corn and woods and gave their attention to Lawton's right and center.

As the 13th Reserves became engaged with Trimble's Brigade, the 5th Reserves, advancing through the eastern part of the East Woods, drove the Confederates out of them and came to the support of the 13th, the right wing of the 5th coming up behind the left of the 13th. The 5th was quickly obliqued beyond the Smoketown road, its right 25 yards from it, and, lining up behind the fence, opened fire upon Trimble's Brigade, in line across the plowed field near the Mumma grave-yard, 300 yards distant. The fighting was severe, the Confederates suffering most, being on open ground, while the Pennsylvanians had the cover of trees. The ammunition of the 13th began to run out, when it was relieved by the 2nd Reserves, which during the night had remained in support to Cooper's Battery, and had before day entered the woods and now moved up to support the 13th. When the 2nd moved up, the 13th fell back for ammunition, but some of the men, having cartridges, remained on the line. Colonel Fisher of the 5th Reserves, observing from his position on lower ground that the left of the 13th had fallen back, and not seeing that the 2nd had taken its place, for it formed more to the right, out of his sight, and supposing that a heavy Confederate fire, heard at this time, had swept the troops from his right, thus exposing that flank, led his regiment off by the left flank, down the east fence of the woods to the big spring at S. Poffenberger's and thence to the Poffenberger woods, bordering the Smoketown road; the 1st, 2nd, and 6th Reserves, and the greater part of the 13th still remaining in the East Woods.

While Trimble's Brigade was engaged with the Pennsylvania Reserves two heavy batteries beyond the Antietam opened fire upon it, and very soon thereafter the Union artillery on the high ground east of D. R. Miller's joined in the fire. Stephen D. Lee now sent two guns of Jordan's Battery to its assistance, but those were soon silenced and withdrawn. Leaving Trimble's Brigade under the severe musketry fire of the 2nd Pennsylvania Reserves and the cross-fire of artillery we note the arrival of reinforcements to Seymour.

When Hooker ordered Ricketts to the support of Seymour he ordered, also, that the batteries of the division should be hurried forward to the high ground between Miller's orchard and the East Woods. Matthew's Battery (F, 1st Pa. Light Artillery) immediately advanced from near S. Poffenberger's woods, passed in rear of the hill where Doubleday's guns were then engaged with Stuart's, and, being fired opened upon by S. D. Lee's guns, went into position near the extreme northwest corner of the East Woods, soon advancing to a more favorable position in the same field, about 30 yards west of the woods, and fired over the corn at Lee's batteries near the church.

Looking toward the Mumma Farm before dawn from the 13th Pennsylvania Reserve's position in the East Woods and along the Smoketown Road. *Author's collection.*

When, at dawn, Ricketts was ordered forward, Hartsuff's and Duryea's [Duryée][3] brigades were directed to flank to the right out of the Poffenberger woods, and then advanced south, Hartsuff, in deployed line, leading Duryée, in column of divisions, in close support on the right. Christian's Brigade was to go directly forward on the left of the Smoketown road. It was daybreak when Hartsuff and Duryée obliqued to the right out of the woods to the grass-fields east of the J. Poffenberger's barn. Hartsuff, who was in line, moved south, but was immediately halted, and Duryée, passing to the right, went through the North Woods and over Magilton's Brigade, lying in them, and halted in a plowed field, where a detail was made from the 105th New York to Thompson's Battery (C, Penn. Light Artillery) which had accompanied the brigade and was short of men. The advance was soon resumed, under a terrific fire of shot and shell from Lee's guns, by which many men were killed and wounded, and passing Matthew's Battery, the brigade went down a gentle incline and deployed along the north fence of Miller's cornfield, about 5:45 a.m., the 107th Pennsylvania on the right, and 97th, 104th, and 105th New York, in order named, on the left, and the 1,100 men laid down.

When Thompson halted his battery for a detail of men Matthews was already engaged. When men were furnished him he opened fire upon S. D. Lee's guns, but finding that Jordan's section, on Trimble's line, had the correct range of his position, he turned his fire upon it until it was withdrawn, and was then ordered to advance and go into action nearly on a line with Matthews and 20 yards east of Miller's orchard and due east of his house. Thompson and Matthews now threw several charges of canister into the cornfield, and then at 6 a.m. Duryée's men sprang to their feet, went over the fence and through very dense corn, standing over their heads, to its south edge—245 yards—the right of the line about 145 yards east of the Hagerstown road, the left about 100 yards from the East Woods. Simultaneously with the advance of Duryée's men into the corn, Thompson's Battery went forward nearly to the fence and again opened upon S. D. Lee's guns.

The south edge of the corn was skirted by a row of broom corn which the men began to poke to the right and left to discover what was in front, the left regiment saw Trimble's Brigade and the right of Lawton's engaged with Seymour's in the East Woods, and the right regiment saw, 230 yards in their front, Lawton's left in rear of a low rail fence, partly thrown down. As Lawton's men had been instructed to watch for the Union line to reach the edge of the corn and for each man to fire down his "own corn row," Duryée's men were instantly fired upon and there was a contest of the most deadly character. At first no attention was paid by either line to the rail

---

[3] Carman misspells Duryée's name as Duryea throughout the manuscript.

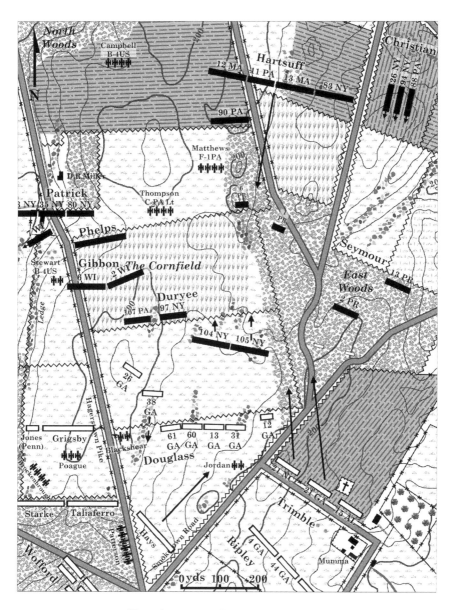

Duryée engages Lawton's Division.

fence in their respective fronts, but each stood and fired on the other, neither party endeavoring to advance, soon, however, the severity of the fire dictated more caution and most of the men, on both sides, laid down and sought cover.

The 105th and 104th New York, on reaching the south edge of the corn pushed out into the open field 160 and 120 yards respectively and were opened upon with such vigor by Lawton's right and the 12th Georgia, and S. D. Lee's guns, that they soon fell back to the corn, the former carrying with it, its mortally wounded commander, Lieutenant Colonel Howard Carroll.

We return to Trimble's Brigade, which we left contending with the 2nd Pennsylvania Reserves and annoyed by artillery fire. The 13th Reserves having been withdrawn and the 5th having retired, because missing the 13th on its right, Walker, commanding Trimble's Brigade, paid particular attention to the 2nd Reserves, which was obliged to fall back a short distance, just as Duryée's men reached the south edge of the corn, upon which Trimble's skirmishers entered the East Woods, but did not penetrate far, as the 2nd Reserves had fallen back a short distance only, to a more advantageous and sheltered position. In the formation of Trimble's Brigade the 12th Georgia, about 100 men, was on the north side of the Smoketown road, its right resting on the road, 20 yards east of the lane running to the Mumma house. In this position it fired at the 2nd Pennsylvania Reserves and the skirmishers of the 1st and 6th. Upon the falling back of the Pennsylvanians and the advance of the 105th and 104th New York, south of the corn, it wheeled to the left and took position behind a rock ledge parallel to the Smoketown road and 100 yards from it, and from this covered position delivered such an accurate fire upon the two regiments that they became much shaken and fell back. Colonel Walker, observing the effect of this cool and deliberate fire, now ordered the 21st Georgia and the 21st North Carolina to wheel to the left, cross the Smoketown road, and, taking shelter under the same low rock-ledge and the swelling ground on either side of it, open fire on the left of Duryée's line with the view of breaking it. The movement was promptly executed and after a few rounds Duryée's left yielded some ground. Observing that General Hays' Louisiana brigade had now come on the field to the support of Lawton and that, apparently, it was going forward to join in the fight, Walker ordered his own line to advance, which it did, a short distance, when, seeing that Hays did not advance with him and that Lawton's right had yielded some ground, thus leaving his own left exposed, and that his men could not advance farther with safety, he fell back to his original position. In this last advance Walker noticed that the 12th Georgia did not go forward with the other regiments, less than a score responding to the order, while the others were seen lying down behind the rock-ledge. Surprised at the conduct of this

Lawton's (Douglass) position from the Smoketown Road behind the brigade. The Cornfield is visible in the background. At the time this modern photo was taken, the eastern half of the Cornfield had been harvested *Author's collection.*

tried and veteran regiment he hastened to it and found that every man had gone forward, who could do so. Those remaining were dead or wounded. Out of 100 men carried into

action 59 were killed or wounded; among the killed was Captain James G. Rodgers, commanding the regiment.

Meanwhile the struggle continued between Duryée's right (the 107th Pennsylvania and 97th New York) and Lawton's left (the 26th, 38th and 61st Georgia). At first the 26th Georgia was 120 yards east of the Hagerstown road, but it obliqued to the left until it gained high ground, about 50 yards from the road and directed a right oblique fire upon the right of the 107th Pennsylvania; the left of the Pennsylvania regiment and the entire 97th New York, being under the fire of the 38th and 61st Georgia. On the west side of the road was Jackson's old division, not yet engaged, but a few of its skirmishers, at the fence of the road, were firing at the flank of the 107th Pennsylvania. The 38th Georgia made a desperate effort to gain the cover of a ledge in its front, near the corn, but was disastrously repulsed; the 61st was content with holding on, suffering terribly from a crossfire. Neither side gained any advantage of ground, but Lawton's men lost more heavily, as they were fired at from both front and right, the fire from Seymour's men in the East Woods enfilading the three left regiments, at the same time Duryée's right partially enfiladed the right regiments. In addition both Lawton's and Trimble's brigades were then, and had been since daybreak, under a distressing artillery fire from the Union batteries in front and from the log range guns beyond the Antietam, which, with the infantry fire, General Early reports: "subjected the two brigades to a terrible fire."

The change of front and advance of the 21st Georgia and the 21st North Carolina caused the 2nd Pennsylvania Reserves and the skirmishers of the 1st and 6th to retire a short distance to a better position, and an incorrect report reached Duryée that they had given way entirely, and that the Confederates were filling the East Woods in pursuit, thus endangering his left flank. Without verifying the report, Duryée, after being in action 30 minutes, ordered his brigade to fall back. These orders met the 105th and 104th New York as they fell back from the pasture field and carried them to the northeast part of the cornfield. Parts of the 97th New York and 107th Pennsylvania followed, but the right of the former and the left of the latter, failing to receive orders, and, from the density of the corn, not perceiving that their comrades had retired, remained a little longer, when it was discovered that they were alone, upon which they fell back through the corn and, at its north side met Hartsuff's Brigade sweeping to the front, and, under Hooker's order they rallied as a support. As these two detachments went back the advance of Doubleday's Division entered the northwest corner of the corn and moved to the attack. In its action of

This small knoll was held by regiments from both Duryée's and Hartsuff's brigades, as well as the 90th Pennsylvania. Photographed both immediately after the battle, and a modern image. The stacked rifles are a monument to the 90th Pennsylvania. *Library of Congress and author's collection.*

about 30 minutes Duryée's Brigade lost 33 1/2 per cent of its number; the most severe loss falling upon the 97th New York; out of 203 present it had 107 killed and wounded, or 52 7/10 per cent.

Immediately upon Duryée's retirement, Lawton's skirmishers pushed into the corn in pursuit, and the entire line, supported by Hays' Brigade, was ordered forward, when it was discovered that the advance of Doubleday's Division, on either side of the Hagerstown road, threatened to turn the left flank, upon which the left of the brigade obliqued toward the road and became engaged with the 6th and 2nd Wisconsin of Doubleday's advance and, at the same time, Jackson's old division, west of the road became engaged. The battle now raged near and along the Hagerstown road and in and west of the East Woods. We shall narrate later the action on the Confederate left of this line, and now resume the narrative of what followed Duryée's withdrawal.

We have stated that while Trimble's Brigade was engaged Hays' Louisiana brigade came on the field. It had bivouacked in the woods northwest of the church. Soon after daylight Lawton ordered Hays to move quickly and fill the interval of 120 yards between the 26th Georgia and the Hagerstown road. Hays crossed the road, 120 yards north of the Dunker Church, and was advancing due north to close the interval, when he was directed by Lawton to bear to the right and take position immediately in rear of his brigade. This was done and he remained in this position until Colonel Douglass commanding Lawton's Brigade, requested him to come to his assistance. With his 550 men he advanced under a deadly fire from Matthews' and Thompson's guns, and was still advancing when Hartsuff's Brigade came down through the cornfield and East Woods and opposed him.

When Hartsuff, after moving out of the Poffenberger woods to the right, at daybreak, halted his brigade, it was that he might go forward and examine the ground over which he was to move and see where Seymour was engaged, and thus lead his men to the most advantageous position for the work in hand. While in the performance of this most important duty he was severely wounded and borne from the field. The command of the brigade devolved upon Colonel Richard Coulter of the 11th Pennsylvania. The delay incident to the halt and change of command was about 30 minutes, but, at the end of that time Coulter had received no orders to advance, and the 90th Pennsylvania, of Christian's Brigade, had been ordered to support Matthews' Battery. When Coulter assumed command the brigade was in line north of the East Woods, in this order from right to left—12th Massachusetts, 11th Pennsylvania, 13th Massachusetts, and 83rd New York. It numbered about 1,000 men. Just as firing began on the Hagerstown road, between the advance of Doubleday's Division and the skirmishers of Jackson's Division, Coulter received orders to go forward and was instantly

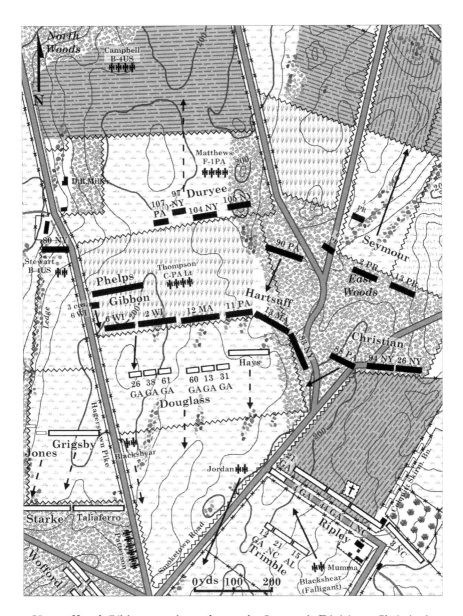

Hartsuff and Gibbon repel an advance by Lawton's Division. Christian's brigade takes up a position on the southern edge of the East Woods. Blackshear's section may have retired earlier.

in motion. He advanced through the East Woods and over the open field west of them, and at Seymour's suggestion obliqued a little to the right to clear Seymour's lines. The 12th Massachusetts, on the right, went down the sloping ground. Lawton's skirmishers had already entered the corn, bullets were flying fast and shells from S. D. Lee's and Stuart's guns were exploding, two companies from the Massachusetts regiment were thrown out, under command of Captain B. F. Cook, and the line continued its advance. As one company of skirmishers was sufficient, the other fell back in with the regiment and Cook went on through the corn, Lawton's skirmishers slowly retiring, the Massachusetts skirmishers falling back into their regiment as it came up. The regiment, Thompson's Battery moving close in its right rear, followed Lawton's men to the south edge of the corn, every step through the corn marked by the dead and wounded from the fire of the Confederate artillery, but there was not a straggler. The regiment advanced about 50 yards beyond the south edge of the corn to a swell of ground trending southwest, then throwing its right 10 or 12 yards farther from the corn than its left, which was about 180 yards from the East Woods. Lawton's main line was not seen until the regiment crowned the knoll and the battle-smoke had drifted away, when it was discovered beyond some low ground, a scattering and irregular line to the right, but more compact in front, and an advancing line was seen on its left front; this was Hays' Brigade and most bloody work began. The 11th Pennsylvania, closely following on the left of the 12th Massachusetts, passed over the 6th Pennsylvania Reserves and through the corn to near its southeast corner, where facing a little west of south it opened fire. On the left the 13th Massachusetts and the 83rd New York swept through the East Woods, and, wheeling to the right, faced nearly west at the edge of the woods, where they became immediately engaged. The entire movement was executed in good order, the regiments coming into position in quick succession and opening fire before fairly halted. From the time the 12th Massachusetts crowned the knoll, south of the corn, to the time the 83rd New York swung around to the edge of the woods, not more than three minutes elapsed, and Hays' Brigade terribly depleted, had reached Lawton's line. Hays did not halt, but pushed right on against the 12th and 13th Massachusetts and 11th Pennsylvania, a part of Lawton's men going with him, the remainder obliquing to the left toward the Hagerstown road, as we shall see, to be repulsed by the 2nd and 6th Wisconsin and parts of Phelps' Brigade.

The weight of Hays' attack fell upon the 12th Massachusetts, 11th Pennsylvania and right wing of the 13th Massachusetts, which were on open ground, much exposed, the left wing of the 13th Massachusetts having the cover of the woods. S. D. Lee's guns tore great gaps in the ranks of the 12th Massachusetts; the musketry fire rapidly thinned it; Major

Looking from the southern edge of the Cornfield toward Lawton's (Douglass) original position just before dawn. Wisps of fog still cover the ground,, to be burned off momentarily with the rising sun, as it did in 1862. *Author's collection.*

Burbank, its commander, was mortally wounded; the colors and the entire color-guard went down in a heap; the men closed up on the colors, which still lay on the ground, and continued their fire. The 11th Pennsylvania and the 13th Massachusetts poured in a deadly fire and, struck in front and flank, Hays and the Georgians, who had had advanced with him, were soon checked, then repulsed and fell back slowly and sullenly to seek cover. At this time Trimble's Brigade, nearly out of ammunition and getting what it could from the cartridge boxes and pockets of the dead and wounded, was barely holding ground, and Lawton's left had been repulsed by Doubleday's advance along the Hagerstown road. While all this was transpiring on the right of Jackson's line, east of the Hagerstown road, bloody work was being done on the left (west) of it, and we now turn our attention to that part of the action.

When Jackson's Division came upon the field, at dusk of the 16th, it was formed in two lines, the brigades of Winder and Jones in first line, on open ground, the right (Winder) resting on the Hagerstown road, on the left of Lawton's Brigade, though separated from it by an interval of 120 yards, Lawton's men not in view, being beyond and below the ridge on which ran the road. The left of the line was about 100 yards from the West Woods. This line of two brigades was under command of Colonel A. J. Grigsby of the 27th Virginia. The second line, the brigades of Starke and Taliaferro, under command of General W. E. Starke, was in the north edge of the southern body of the West Woods, 210 yards in rear of the first line, Taliaferro's Brigade resting its right on the Hagerstown road, Starke, on the left, extending to the west edge of the woods. These four brigades comprised the "Stonewall" Division, commanded by General John R. Jones.

The greater part of Jackson's artillery did not enter the West Woods, but was in the open ground west of them, near the A. Poffenberger barn, but Poague's, Brockenbrough's and D'Aquin's batteries followed the infantry and took position, Poague's on Grigsby's line, Brockenbrough's in front of Starke's Brigade and D'Aquin's near Brockenbrough's. Before the action had fairly opened Jackson saw that D'Aquin was in a very exposed position, where, after the infantry became engaged, he could not use his guns to advantage, and ordered him out of the woods to the open ground on the west to act with Stuart's cavalry. Poague, who had done some work, at dusk of the 16th, sent back his two 10-pound Parrott guns and was given two howitzers from Raine's Battery, and, at daybreak of the 17th had three guns a few feet in advance of Grigsby's line and about 35 yards west of the Hagerstown road. Skirmishers were well out in front from D. R. Miller's on the right to beyond the Nicodemus house on the left. The strength of Jackson's old division was about 1,600 men. General John R. Jones says:

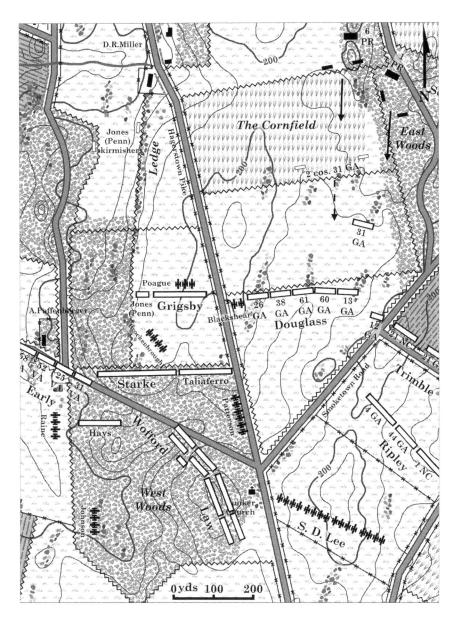

The initial position of Jackson's Division.

Regiments were commanded by captains and lieutenants and some companies by sergeants. Many of the men had shoes and many went into action barefooted. They were ragged, tired, hungry and barefooted, but they were soldiers who had marched hundreds of miles during the summer and fought many battles under Jackson and Lee, and upon this field fought with a gallantry never surpassed and rarely equaled.

At daybreak an artillery duel began across Jackson's front between Doubleday's and Stuart's guns, and soon after daybreak a stream of round shot and shell came from Matthews' and Thompson's batteries on the Miller farm; and from the heavy guns beyond the Antietam came a fire which enfiladed Jackson's Division and took it in reverse. Poague's and Brockenbrough's guns replied to the guns on the right front, but Brockenbrough was soon ordered to retire through the West Woods. During the artillery fire General John R. Jones, commanding the division, was stunned by the explosion of a shell over his head and obliged to turn over the command to General Starke and leave the field. Lawton and Trimble were now at work on the right and very soon Doubleday's advance was seen marching on the east of and close to the Hagerstown road.

Before this Grigsby had noticed the gap between his right and Lawton's left and had called attention to it, and when Doubleday was seen advancing, he again sent a member of his staff to Starke with the request that the gap be filled at once. It was just at this time that Lawton's order came to the same effect and Jackson, who was with Starke, ordered Hays to move through the woods in Starke's rear, cross the road and fill the gap; at the same time Early was ordered to the left to support Stuart's cavalry and the artillery on Nicodemus hill. How Hays executed his orders has been told; what Early did shall be told later; we now follow Doubleday.

It was nearly 9 o'clock, on the night of the 16th, when Doubleday's Division, infantry and artillery, went into bivouac on the hill north of Joseph Poffenberger's. At very early daybreak Doubleday galloped along the line and ordered Gibbon and Phelps to move their brigades back at once, as they were on a hillside, in open range of the Confederate batteries on Nicodemus hill, about a 1,000 yards distant. The men, most of whom were in sound sleep, were awakened, and Gibbon hurriedly began moving back from the exposed slope. He had moved not more than ten rods when a shell burst over his brigade, then another, followed by a percussion shell, which struck a threshing machine and exploded in the center of the moving mass, killing three men and wounding 11 of the 6th Wisconsin, and disabling some men of other regiments. Moving on the brigade soon reached the shelter of the Poffenberger barn. This fire came from the batteries of Balthis and Wooding, on Stuart's line, and was the first artillery

Nicodemus Hill seen from the north. The Confederate guns would have faced to the left. *Author's collection.*

firing on the morning of the 17th of September. The first shot was probably fired by Balthis' Staunton battery, commanded by Lieutenant A. W. Garber. Carpenter immediately joined his fire to that of Garber and Wooding, and they were promptly answered by Doubleday's guns, the first shot killing Lieutenant-Colonel John T. Thornton, commanding 3rd Virginia Cavalry, who was in rear of Nicodemus hill, where Fitz-Hugh Lee had moved the greater part of his cavalry brigade, and on the west slope of the hill Jackson slept during the night of the 16th.

This was the artillery prelude to the battle of Antietam, and was soon followed by S. D. Lee's guns near the Dunker Church, the guns beyond the Antietam, Poague's and Brockenbrough's guns and those of Matthews and Thompson.

The Confederate guns on Nicodemus hill were soon silenced, but resumed their fire soon after, not upon Doubleday's artillery alone but upon his infantry and that of Ricketts and Meade's divisions, as they moved to the front, an enfilading fire which was very annoying and that inflicted some loss. The fire from these guns ranged into the ranks of the 3rd Pennsylvania Cavalry, which had bivouacked near the East Woods, causing it to change position. The regiment was then broken up into detachments, serving on different parts of the field, supporting batteries and gathering stragglers.

It was after the opening of this artillery fire that Doubleday was directed to get ready to move. He had previously dispatched Gibbon to take the advance, followed in order by Phelps, Patrick, and Hofmann. It was nearing 6 a.m., when Hooker ordered the advance, Gibbon to begin the attack along the Hagerstown road, followed by Phelps as a support. About 15 minutes later Patrick went forward by Hooker's order, and by the same order Hofmann remained to support the artillery, on the Poffenberger hill in his rear.

Gibbon's Brigade consisted of the 19th Indiana, 2nd, 6th and 7th Wisconsin. It numbered 971 officers and men. It was a staunch organization, known as the "Iron Brigade," and had a good soldier as its commander. Gibbon advanced in column of divisions, the 6th Wisconsin, Lieutenant Colonel Edward S. Bragg, on the right, on the east of the Hagerstown road, through the North Woods, which were being vigorously shelled by Stuart's guns, over Magilton's Brigade of Pennsylvania Reserves, and into the open field south of the woods, where Hooker was directing affairs. Here the 6th Wisconsin was deployed in line and two companies thrown out as skirmishers. Under Hooker's orders the regiment, followed by the brigade, obliqued to the right until it reached the road, then marched south. Upon approaching D. R. Miller's garden the fire from this point was severe, the enemy still holding it as a picket post, although Duryée had passed it on the east. The skirmishers, under Captain John A. Kellogg,

Brigadier General John Gibbon.
Library of Congress.

drove the Confederates out, and the regiment pushed on over the open field, which was swept by an artillery fire from Stuart's guns on the right and Poague's in front. The right wing passed to the right of Miller's garden without trouble; the left was delayed in its advance by a picket fence surrounding the garden. In moving over the flower beds and through the rose bushes Captain E. A. Brown was killed by a musket ball. Beyond the garden, in a peach orchard, the two wings of the regiment were united, just as the Confederate skirmishers disappeared into the cornfield, which was on rising ground, the cornstalks standing thick and high. This was the western part of the Miller cornfield. Bragg did not linger in the peach orchard but ordered the regiment forward. It climbed the south fence of the orchard, moved across a shallow basin of 75 yards and pushed into the corn. The three right companies were crowded into the road and across it on the right. The other regiments of the brigade followed the 6th Wisconsin and halted, closed in mass, in the open space between the orchard and the cornfield, while the Wisconsin skirmishers were searching the corn.

Campbell's Battery followed Gibbon through the North Woods and halted about 100 yards south of them, and a section, under Lieutenant James Steuart [Stewart], was advanced and opened fire over the heads of the infantry, in reply to S. D. Lee's and Poague's guns and, also, upon the woods north of the Dunker Church. Reynolds' New York battery was subsequently ordered to the same field, and the position on the plateau north of Poffenberger's, was filled by Cooper's and Simpson's batteries of Meade's Division.

Phelps' Brigade followed Campbell's Battery through the North Woods and into the open field in which Hooker and staff were seen, directly in the rear of Campbell's Battery, and was ordered by Hooker to move by the flank through the field and support Gibbon, who was seen advancing. The direct and cross artillery fire over the field was very heavy, but the brigade moved without loss to a point some 90 yards in advance of and on the right of the battery, the right resting on the Hagerstown road, and the line moved forward some 50 yards in rear of Gibbon. Phelps had five regiments the 22nd, 24th, 30th, and 84th New York (14th Brooklyn) and 2nd United States Sharpshooters. The brigade numbered 425 officers and men.

Patrick's Brigade consisted of the 21st, 23rd, 35th, and 80th New York, and numbered about 824 men. It followed Phelps through the North Woods, open field and peach orchard, halting in the shallow depression between the orchard and the cornfield, as the 6th Wisconsin became engaged, closely supported by the rest of its brigade and Phelps.

We left the 6th Wisconsin advancing into the cornfield. Its skirmishers soon found the enemy mostly along the fence bordering the Hagerstown road and under cover, these were rapidly driven across the road and the regiment moved up steadily in support, closely followed by the 2nd

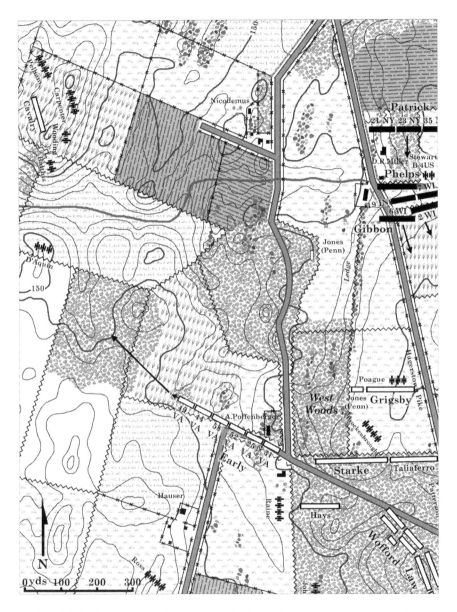

Doubleday's division advances south along the Hagerstown Turnpike.
Early's Brigade moves west to support the artillery on Nicodemus heights.

Wisconsin, the right of the 6th on and to the right of the road, under the immediate command of Bragg, the left in the corn, under Major R. R. Dawes.

For some reason the right of the skirmish line failed to advance and clear that flank or discover what was in that direction, and the right wing reached a rise of ground in front of Miller's barn and some straw stacks on the right of the road, when it received an unexpected and severe fire upon the flank from Captain A. C. Page's Virginia skirmishers, lying along the edge of the West Woods, nearly opposite the barn, and also under the cover of the rock ledge between the road and the woods.

At this moment a Confederate gun, probably of Cutts' Battalion, passed into the road, in front, and Bragg ordered Captain Bachelle's company, which was in the road, to advance to a ridge, crossing the road a few yards in front, and open fire upon the horses attached to the guns; at the same [sic] he ordered the two companies on the right of the road to advance and occupy a shallow basin between two swells of ground, and a few yards nearer the enemy, whom he had not yet seen, but of whose near presence he was well assured. So soon as this advance was attempted the fire from the West Woods and the ledge upon his flank increased to a murderous enfilade, a fire from a skirmish line in front followed and, looking in that direction, Bragg saw Grigsby's line, the brigades of Winder and Jones, lying along the fence and across the field to the West Woods, and at right angles to the road. No sooner had he discovered it than the entire line rose to its feet and poured in a volley which struck down many of his men and swept over the field and into the cornfield held by the left companies. This rendered advance on the right impracticable and Bachelle's company, in the road, was ordered to lie down under the corner of the fence. No sooner had he given the order than Bragg received a severe and painful wound in the left arm, but was still able to direct the right companies to draw back under cover of the road fence, and the left wing to halt and lie down in the corn. These orders were being executed when he fainted and was carried to the rear, Major Dawes succeeding to command.

Early in the morning Poague's Virginia battery of three guns was a few yards in front of Grigsby's Virginians and was soon vigorously engaged with the Union batteries of Matthews and Thompson, and then with Stewart's two guns; it directed some of its fire upon Doubleday's advancing brigades, also upon Duryée and Hartsuff. When the skirmishers became engaged and Gibbon's line advanced through the corn, Poague withdrew to the rear of Grigsby's line and threw a few rounds of canister into the corn; when the Wisconsin companies appeared, marching west of the road, the Union artillery, Stewart's guns now assisting, still keeping up a rapid and precise fire, he fell back to the A. Poffenberger barn. Grigsby held on with his less than 450 men, subjected to the same destructive artillery fire, and to

Brigadier General John R. Jones Division's initial position west of the Hagerstown Turnpike from the Union lines. They were lined up in front of the far wood line. *Author's collection.*

the severe fire of the Wisconsin skirmishers, who, creeping up along the fences of the road, did effective work upon his weak line. His men were falling fast, his left was threatened by the advance of a Union force through the West Woods, and he sent Lieutenant J. M. Garnett, of his staff, to Starke, with the message that he could not hold on much longer. Garnett found Starke in the edge of the woods, delivered the message, and as he lifted his eyes he saw the men retreating across the open field. Grigsby had used all efforts to hold on, but the fire upon him was so destructive, that Major H. J. Williams, commanding 5th Virginia, suggested to him to move back into the woods. Grigsby would not take the responsibility, upon which Williams ordered the 5th Virginia to fall back and the other regiments of Winder's Brigade followed; once started the retreat was rapid.

Jones' Brigade, commanded by Captain John E. Penn, 42nd Virginia, was on the left of Winder's and quickly followed it in retreat. The left of this brigade rested about 100 yards from the West Woods; it was very small and the greater part of it, under command of Captain A. C. Page, was on the skirmish line. When Gibbon was seen advancing through the D. R. Miller's fields, the advance skirmishers, near Nicodemus's, were recalled and the greater part of them posted in the east edge of the West Woods, some of them were advanced to the shelter of the rock ledge running south from Miller's barn, and it was this body of skirmishers that opened fire upon Gibbon's flank as he advanced along the road and through the corn, which fire, with the direct fire of Grigsby in front, caused the 6th Wisconsin to halt and Gibbon to order the deployment of the 19th Indiana and 7th Wisconsin to the right of the road and down to the West Woods. At the same time Gibbon ordered Stewart's two guns to the front, and at about the same moment Doubleday ordered Patrick, who had come up five minutes before, to cross the road and support the movement of the 19th Indiana and 7th Wisconsin. The 19th Indiana crossed the Hagerstown road between D. R. Miller's house and barn and formed line; Captain W. W. Dudley, deploying his company as skirmishers, quickly dislodged the Virginians from their cover at the rock ledge, and pushed on into the northern part of the West Woods, the Virginians falling back, Dudley closely following about 120 yards into the woods, when, the opposition becoming very pronounced, he halted; the regiment, slowly following the skirmishers, halted at the edge of the woods, where the 7th Wisconsin came up and formed on its left, at the extreme northeast corner of the woods, and sent a company of skirmishers to assist Dudley. Patrick's Brigade followed the 7th Wisconsin across the road and formed in the rear of it and the 19th Indiana. The 19th Indiana and the 7th Wisconsin now pushed into the woods; Dudley again went forward; Captain Page, who had been forced back, was now reinforced by Captain Penn, who had been specially charged with the care of that flank, but Penn was soon severely wounded, losing a

Looking south along the rock ledge from the Miller barn. *Author's collection.*

leg, and the Virginians fell back to their brigade line, just as Winder's was withdrawing, and Jones' Brigade, now under command of Captain Page, quickly followed; the two brigades reduced to less than 250 men, obliquing to the right in retiring and rallying in the woods in rear of Starke's left.

As the 19th Indiana and 7th Wisconsin were sweeping through the West Woods the 2nd Wisconsin was moving in the corn to the left of the 6th Wisconsin. As it came up to the 6th, Lieutenant Colonel Allen, commanding the 2nd, directed Dawes to advance. Dawes ordered his men up and, guiding on the right of the 2nd Wisconsin, swung away from the road, ordering Captain Kellogg, on the right, to move the right companies obliquely to the left in the corn. Kellogg ordered his men up, but so many were shot down that he ordered them down again at once. The line did not wait for Kellogg but pushed on through the corn, followed by Phelps' Brigade, 25 yards in rear, and, farther to the left, Hartsuff's Brigade was sweeping through the east part of the corn and the East Woods. Up to this time the 2nd Wisconsin had not given or received a shot, nor had it seen an enemy, but, as it reached the south edge of the corn, the men saw before them, the left of Lawton's Brigade, about 200 yards distant. There was no time for extended observations, for, as the 2nd Wisconsin and the seven companies of the 6th came into view, the 26th, 38th, and 61st Georgia rose from the ground and simultaneously both lines opened fire. There was but a short halt at the south edge of the corn, the Wisconsin men went over the fence bounding it; Kellogg came up the road with his three companies, and all went forward, firing and shouting, driving back and to the left the three Georgia regiments, to the foot of the high ground, where, only a skirmish line now, and under cover, they held on until Hood came up. This encounter near the road was at the time Hays came up farther to the Confederate right and made the charge in which most of the officers in both his own and Lawton's Brigade were killed or wounded.

At the moment the Georgians were driven back by the Wisconsin men, the latter saw a body of Confederates swarming out of the West Woods, just north of the church, as though intent on turning the right of the Union line, upon which Colonel Allen, on the left, changed front obliquely to the right to secure a better position for firing and directed his men to construct a rail barricade. This was on the high ground near the road, and his line faced southwest. The 6th Wisconsin formed on his right, its three right companies still in the road, many of the men lying down under cover of the fence.

The advancing Confederate line was Starke's, composed of his own brigade and that of Taliaferro; Starke's Brigade numbering about 650 men, Taliaferro's about 500. When Starke received Grigsby's appeal for help his line was lying down in the woods, about 20 yards from the edge, Taliaferro's right resting on the Hagerstown road. Starke immediately

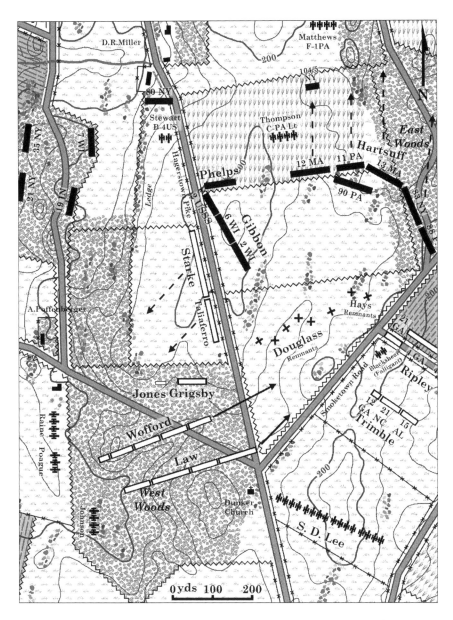

The brigades of Starke and Taliaferro leave the West Woods and engage Doubleday along the Hagerstown Turnpike, only to be driven back after a brutal fight. Hood's Division begins to move out of the West Woods to support what's left of Lawton's division.

ordered the men up, waited until Grigsby's men had fallen back out of the way, then sprang to the front and led the advance, his objective being the southwestern corner of the Miller cornfield, where the Wisconsin men had made their appearance in pursuit of the Georgians. He led his own brigade obliquely to the right and as Taliaferro's charged directly to the front, the right of one and the left of the other, becoming mixed, causing some confusion, but both brigades pressed obliquely to the right; soon received the fire of the Wisconsin men, Starke was mortally wounded (dying within an hour) about 160 yards north of the woods and 140 yards west of the road, and the two brigades, under a murderous fire, thinning its ranks at every step, reached the high and strong post and rail fence of the road and came face to face with the Wisconsin men across the road, only 30 to 75 yards away. Fire was immediately opened; the 14th Brooklyn of Phelps' Brigade, rushed out of the corn and merged with the Wisconsin men, and the fighting was fast, furious, and deadly. The Union men fell on all parts of the line, some ran back into the corn. Lieutenant Colonel Allen was wounded, and after a few minutes, the Union men fell back and laid down below the low rail fence, at the edge of the corn, but only for a moment, and the Confederates began to climb the fence into the road. Phelps, as we have seen, had moved up to within 25 yards of the Wisconsin men, before they had left the corn and, after they had gone forward and become engaged with Starke, the 14th Brooklyn rushed to their assistance. About the same time the 2nd U.S. Sharpshooters moved up to the fence and laid down. Colonel Phelps reports: "Having ascertained that the enemy's line was formed with their left advanced...and that they were in position to partially enfilade our line, I ordered the 2nd U.S. Sharpshooters, Colonel Post, to move to the right and front, advancing his left, and to engage the enemy at that point." Post went over the fence and about 30 yards beyond it, his right on or very near the Hagerstown road, his left thrown forward, thus making an oblique line with the road, and engaged the left of Starke's line (the 1st Louisiana), in and beyond the road. The Wisconsin men and 14th Brooklyn were slowly falling back when Post was taking this position, they quickly rallied in the corn and with the remainder of Phelps' Brigade again went forward, formed on the left of the Sharpshooters and renewed the fight. Meanwhile some of the Confederates had climbed the fence and got into the road and others were following, but the Union fire was so severe that no farther advance was attempted, but they held on to the line of the fence, though suffering severely, and the contest had been maintained some 15 minutes when new trouble came to them.

It will be remembered that, when the advance of the 6th Wisconsin was checked by the fire on its right flank, Gibbon ordered Stewart with his two guns to the front, from his position east of the Miller house, and the 19th Indiana, 7th Wisconsin, and Patrick's Brigade to the right in and near the

Confederate dead along the western fence of the Hagerstown Turnpike looking north, most likely Louisianans from Starke's Brigade. At times, the Union line was just on the other side of the road along the opposite fence.

Library of Congress.

West Woods, where they drove back the Virginia skirmishers of Jones' Brigade. Stewart moved very promptly, came down the road at a dead run and, wheeling to the right, put his two guns in position in front of some straw stacks south of the Miller barn, and his limbers in rear of the stacks and between them and the barn to protect his horses. He was now ordered to move forward about 150 yards to the summit of the high ground, but objected, as he could see Starke's men coming out of the woods, and the advanced position would bring him under their close fire, however, he went forward about 50 yards and came into battery about 30 yards west of the road. At the same time the 80th New York (135 men) of Patrick's Brigade came to his support, its right wing in rear of the guns, while the left wing, under Major J. B. Hardenbergh, advanced down the field close to the road. As the ground was undulating and not favorable for the use of canister Stewart opened fire upon Starke's men with spherical case, the left of the 80th New York fired a few shots upon the left flank of the 1st Louisiana, the skirmishers of the 19th Indiana were seen cautiously coming up on the left and rear, and Starke's entire line retired rapidly, but in pretty good order, by the right flank, to the woods from which it had advanced, Stewart's shrapnel following it.

At the moment of retiring the color bearer of the 1st Louisiana was killed at the fence, the colors were seen to drop over the fence into the road, and Adjutant Louis C. Parmelee and others of the Sharpshooters rushed forward to seize them, received a galling fire from the left, by which Parmelee was killed, but another secured the colors. Many of the Sharpshooters crossed both fences of the road in eager pursuit of the Louisianians, some went down the road, but the greater part of the line, the Wisconsin men and Phelps' New York men, moved down the east side and were rapidly approaching the Dunker Church, when out from the woods around the church and into the open ground on the east swept Hood's Division, and delivered such a business like fire that the pursuing forces halted, then fell back in some disorder, those on the left to the corn, while the Sharpshooters, flanked on the left and nearly surrounded, were crowded into the road, along which they retreated to D. R. Miller's. The left wing of the 80th New York fell back and joined its right wing in rear of Stewart's guns.

Starke's men had been less than 30 minutes engaged and lost heavily. Starke and nine other officers of the brigade were killed. Colonels Williams, Stafford and Pendleton succeeded each other quickly in command, all being wounded, and of the 650 carried into action nearly 300 were killed and wounded. Taliaferro's Brigade lost heavily; two officers commanding it were wounded, and of the 500 carried into action about 170 were killed and wounded. The Union loss was less heavy.

A close-up view of Confederate dead along the Hagerstown pike. The proximity of the fence on the opposite side of the road is clearly evident, a testimony to the savage close range engagement that at times occurred here. *Library of Congress.*

The moment has now come to note the movement of Hood's Division, but, before accompanying it in its brilliant and bloody advance, it is desirable to see in what position and condition the Union lines are to meet it.

The 19th Indiana and 7th Wisconsin, after having pushed into the West Woods and driven out the Virginians, with Patrick's Brigade held the north part of the Woods and the rock-ledge running south from Miller's barn. Hofmann's Brigade remained in position supporting the division batteries on the Poffenberger hill, which had silenced the Confederate batteries on Nicodemus hill and compelled most of them to be withdrawn. Matthews', Reynolds' and four of Campbell's guns are in the field between D. R. Miller's and the East Woods, the brigades of Magilton and Anderson, with Ransom's Battery, are moving from the North Woods to the front, and Christian's Brigade had moved up in close support to Seymour and Hartsuff, who are still engaged in the southeast corner of the cornfield and in the East Woods.

Christian's Brigade was composed of the 26th and 94th New York, 88th and 90th Pennsylvania. Very early in the morning the 90th Pennsylvania was detached to support Matthews' Battery, in the field west of the north part of the East Woods, and the other three regiments moved out of the S. Poffenberger woods and formed line south of them. After a halt of some minutes they were formed in column of division and advanced toward the East Woods, did an unnecessary amount of drilling, under a wicked artillery fire, that killed and wounded many men and demoralized one or two of the most prominent officers, and again halted near the East Woods. After a few minutes they were ordered to advance and support Hartsuff, then severely engaged; they entered the woods and again halted. Seymour now rode up and ordered the regiments to deploy in line and go forward. The 26th and 94th New York, moving south through the woods, crossed the Smoketown road, the 26th was on the left. As the two regiments made their appearance at the fence they were greeted by a charge of canister from a battery about midway between Mumma's and the Smoketown road, and by a fire from Ripley's Brigade, which had now moved up on Trimble's right, and was in line near the grave yard and along the fence of a cornfield to its right. The two regiments opened fire, not only upon Ripley, but upon Trimble's men, also, who could be seen behind the fences of the Smoketown road, engaging the left of Hartsuff's line, the 83rd New York, now assisted by the 88th Pennsylvania. Some Pennsylvania Reserves were still in the line and carefully firing, but Christian's advance had relieved the 1st and 2nd Reserves, which now fell out of the woods.

When Christian's three regiments went into position men of the 88th Pennsylvania saw to the right and front Lawton and Hays engaged with Hartsuff, and still farther to the front could be seen fighting on the

The Mumma farm from the perspective of Christian's brigade, and earlier, the 5th Pennsylvania Reserves. The Mumma farm lane is just behind the crest of the hill to the right. *Author's collection.*

Hagerstown road, between Gibbon's and Phelps' men on one side and Starke's on the other. S. D. Lee's guns were searching the East Woods with round shot and shell and firing over the heads of Lawton and Hays at the Union batteries north of the cornfield, and a little later could be seen Hood's advance from the church, and on the left both the 26th and 94th New York saw a Confederate column (Colquitt's Brigade) the heads of the men visible only, marching by 4's toward the right, through the low ground south of the Mumma house, then in flames, and the hour was 7 o'clock.

While Christian's three regiments were going into position on the left, the right and center of Hartsuff's Brigade were melting away under the persistent and fatal fire of Hays and Lawton, who, although repulsed, were still holding on, waiting for help. The 12th Massachusetts had been reduced to less than 40 men, the 11th Pennsylvania had suffered terribly, all were short of ammunition, and Colonel Coulter rode into the East Woods looking for help, and, as he entered them, met the 90th Pennsylvania moving to join its brigade. It had been in support of Matthews' Battery since early morning. Coulter asked Colonel Lyle, commanding the regiment to come to his assistance, Lyle at once brought his regiment into line, passed out of the woods and over the ground held by the 13th Massachusetts, and swept into the pasture field about 160 yards west of the woods and 60 yards south of the corn, planted the colors on a rock ledge and, facing southwest, opened fire upon Hays and Lawton, and, while so engaged, saw a Union body near the Hagerstown road, go forward, then fall back.

During the not more than 30 minutes it had been engaged Hartsuff's Brigade suffered greatly. The 12th Massachusetts carried into action, according to Fox, in his *Regimental Losses*, 334 officers and men, and had 49 killed, 165 wounded and 10 missing, an aggregate of 224, or 67 per cent of those engaged. When it saw help coming the colors were raised from the ground, where they had fallen, dead color bearers under them and over them, and 32 men marched with them to the rear. The 11th Pennsylvania had 235 officers and men in action, and lost 125 killed and wounded, over 53 per cent. The losses in the 13th Massachusetts and 83rd New York were severe, but not in such proportions to numbers engaged.

The right and center of Hartsuff's Brigade having fallen back, the Confederates now gave their undivided attention to the 90th Pennsylvania. As the 12th Massachusetts fell back it saw the advance of Hood's men from the woods at the church and the 4th Alabama, marching by the flank down the Smoketown road, and the 90th Pennsylvania saw the same, and Thompson's Battery, still in the cornfield, opened upon them with shrapnel, it could not use canister because so many Union wounded lay close in front of the guns.

View of Hays' counterattack from Hartsuff's brigade position. The 11th and 90th Pennsylvania, and 13th Massachusetts, fought in this area. Hay's approached from the open ground to the left. *Author's collection.*

Soon after the retirement of the three right regiments of Hartsuff, the 83rd New York fell back, and, very soon thereafter, as everything on the right had gone and Hood's line was advancing, the 88th Pennsylvania was given orders to retire. Many protested and would have remained but the order was repeated and the regiment fell back. Meanwhile the 26th and 94th New York, on the extreme left, east of the Smoketown road, were keeping up a desultory fire upon Trimble's and Ripley's men, but soon the 94th New York saw that the 88th Pennsylvania, on its right, had gone, Hood's men were still advancing, the 4th Alabama was seen coming down the road from the church, and the regiment fell back in some confusion, closely followed by the 26th New York, which had gradually melted away, a few only remaining to retire as Ripley's men began to advance and the 4th Alabama approached the woods on the right. There was nothing now left south of the east part of the cornfield to resist Hood's advance, but the 90th Pennsylvania.

As the Confederate brigades of Trimble, Lawton, and Hays, did no more fighting after Hood's advance had relieved them, we may anticipate their withdrawal and count their losses. Walker, commanding Trimble's Brigade, who had been painfully wounded, and unfitted for further duty, ordered the commandants of regiments to conduct them to the rear to replenish ammunition and collect the stragglers. Captain Rodgers, commanding 12th Georgia, and Captain Miller, commanding 21st North Carolina, were killed, Major Glover, commanding 21st Georgia, severely wounded, and of the less than 700 carried by the brigade into action 237 were killed, wounded, and missing. Lawton's Brigade went off the field without a commander; when in the fields in the rear Major John H. Lowe, 31st Georgia, finding that he was senior officer, reformed it. Colonel Douglass its commander had been killed in the last charge; Major A. P. McRae, commanding 61st Georgia, and Captain W. H. Battey, commanding the 38th were killed, three regimental commanders were wounded, and nearly all the company commanders of the brigade killed or wounded, and 567, or one half of the brigade, killed, wounded, or missing. The 38th Georgia carried 123 officers and men into action, and lost 70 killed and wounded. In its gallant fight Hays' Brigade suffered terribly, losing 60 per cent in killed and wounded, both Hays' staff officers were disabled, Colonel H. B. Strong and five other officers of the 6th Louisiana, and five more officers of the brigade were dead on the field. Every regimental commander was either killed or wounded. Hays gathered the small remnant of his brigade after they had fallen back to the West Woods and conducted them farther to the rear. None of these three brigades were again engaged during the day.

About the time Hays made his advance and was repulsed, General Lawton, commanding the division, was wounded and borne from the field.

Dead horse west of the East Woods. Reliable circumstantial evidence points to it belonging to Colonel Henry B. Strong of the 6th Louisiana, who was killed in this area.[4] *Library of Congress.*

---

[4] William A. Frassanito, *Antietam: The Photographic Legacy of America's Bloodiest Day* (Gettysburg: Thomas Publications, 1978), pp. 122-125.

General Early, who succeeded to the command of Lawton's Division officially reports:

> The terrible nature of the conflict in which those three brigades had been engaged, and the steadiness with which they maintained their position are shown by the losses they sustained. They did not retire from the field until Gen. Lawton had been wounded and borne from the field, Col. Douglass, commanding Lawton's Brigade, had been killed, and the brigades had sustained a loss of 554 killed and wounded out of 1,150, losing five regimental commanders out of 6; Hays' Brigade had sustained a loss of 323 out of 550, including every regimental commander and all his staff, and Col. Walker and one of his staff had been disabled, and the brigade he was commanding had sustained a loss of 228 out of less than 700 present, including 3 out of 4 regimental commanders.

General Hooker reports, "The slain lay in rows precisely as they had stood in their ranks a few minutes before. It was never my fortune to witness a more bloody, dismal battlefield."

General Jackson, in his official report, says:

> About sunrise the Federal infantry advanced in heavy force to the edge of the edge of the wood on the eastern side of the turnpike, driving in our skirmishers. Batteries were opened in front from the wood with shell and canister, and our troops became exposed for near an hour to a terrific storm of shell, canister, and musketry. With heroic spirit our lines advanced to the conflict and maintained their position, in the face of superior numbers, with stubborn resolution, sometimes driving the enemy before them and sometimes being compelled to fall back before their well-sustained and destructive fire. Fresh troops from time to time relieved the enemy's ranks, and the carnage on both sides was terrific.

In the midst of this terrific carnage Hood came into action and added one half his division to the ghastly roster of dead and wounded. Hood's Division consisted of two brigades commanded by Colonel W. T. Wofford, 18th Georgia, and Colonel E. M. Law, 4th Alabama. Wofford's was Hood's old command, generally known as the Texas Brigade, comprising the 1st, 4th and 5th Texas, 18th Georgia, and the Hampton (S. C.) Legion. Law's Brigade consisted of the 4th Alabama, 6th North Carolina, 2nd and 11th Mississippi. The division numbered about 2,000 men, their superior fighting quality not excelled in the army. Up to this day they had never known

Brigadier General John B. Hood. Photographed later in the war.
Library of Congress.

defeat. Hood was a lion-hearted soldier; his brigade commanders brave and skillful officers.

When Hood was relieved by Lawton, on the night of the 16th, and retired to the woods about 250 yards in rear of the Dunker Church, it was to get food for his men, who had been nearly famished for three days, and he rode in search of his wagons. It was with much difficulty that he found these in the darkness, and they contained flour only. Not until nearly dawn was this in the hands of his men and they were without cooking utensils. It was dawn before the dough was prepared, which the men proceeded to cook on ramrods. About 4 a.m. Hood sent his aide to General D. H. Hill, apprising him of his condition and asking if he could furnish any troops to assist in holding the position on the left, to which Hill replied that he could not. As we have seen, the fighting began at dawn, in and near the East Woods, and, soon thereafter, Hood received notice from Lawton that he would require all the assistance he could give him, and later, when Hartsuff and Gibbon advanced, an officer of Lawton's staff dashed up to Hood, saying "General Lawton sends his compliments, with the request that you come at once to his support" and added that Lawton had been wounded. "To Arms" was instantly sounded, and quite a number of Hood's men were obliged to go to the front, leaving their uncooked rations behind; some carried the half-cooked dough on their ramrods and ate it as they went forward.

At this time the Union artillery fire was very heavy from the batteries north of the cornfield, as well as those beyond the Antietam, the latter fire directed at S. D. Lee's guns, but going over them and into the woods around the church. Shot and shell fell into the ranks of the division, killing and wounding many men, but it quickly formed and went through the woods and to the Hagerstown road, under a heavy fire of shrapnel, shell and round shot, and thence into the clover field nearly opposite the Dunker Church. Law, on the right, went out by the flank. After crossing the road he threw his brigade into line, facing northeast, and gave the order to advance, his objective point being that portion of the East Woods south of the cornfield. The 4th Alabama, being crowded out of line, moved by the flank on the Smoketown road. From right to left the regiments were in this order: 4th Alabama, 6th North Carolina, 2nd and 11th Mississippi. On reaching field Law saw but few Confederates, these were in much confusion, without commanders, but still fighting with much determination.

Wofford's Texas Brigade moved through the woods and across the Hagerstown road, about 100 yards north of the church, and formed up on Law's left almost if not quite as soon as Law had formed line, and faced nearly north. It was a general complaint against the Texas Brigade that it fought too fast, whether well founded or not we do not know, but we do know that on this occasion no sooner had it cleared the woods than it

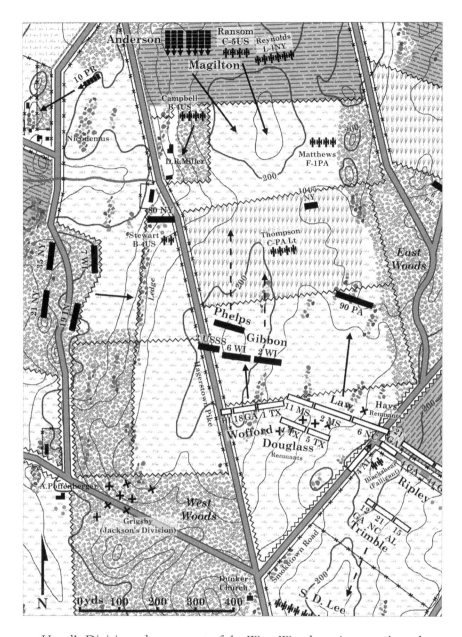

Hood's Division advances out of the West Woods, swings north, and charges into the Cornfield. The 19th Indiana and 7th Wisconsin advance to the shelter of the ledge west of the Hagerstown Turnpike.
Carman's text, used here, puts the 11th Mississippi on the brigade left, but all the Carman-Cope maps put the 2nd Mississippi on the left.

opened fire upon the two Wisconsin regiments and Phelps' men, who were following Starke's defeated and retreating command. In moving across the road the brigade was thus formed from right to left: 5th, 4th and 1st Texas, 18th Georgia and Hampton Legion. Hood says that as he moved across the road in front of the church: "Lawton was borne to the rear on a litter, his command was dispersed or fighting in small groups, behind such shelter of rocks and ledges, as the open field south of the corn afforded, and the only organized body of Confederate troops left upon that part of the field, were some 40 men who had rallied around the gallant Harry Hays, on the highest ground near the junction of the cornfield and the meadow"; and these were anxiously awaiting Hood's arrival. Hood crossed the Hagerstown road at 7 o'clock.[5]

There was no halting the division when the open field was reached for now the ranks were plowed with artillery fire. Thompson, who was in the cornfield, opened upon them with spherical case as soon as he saw the leading regiment emerge from the woods; Matthews, who was on the higher ground, fired over the heads of Hartsuff's men, who were just retiring, and the guns beyond the Antietam dropped heavy shell among them. They pressed on, unable to answer the musketry fire, which was now striking them, for Hays and some of the Georgians were still in front, and the dense smoke prevented a clear view of the enemy.

Meanwhile Hood had ridden to the front and finding that Hays was out of ammunition and his brigade practically destroyed or dispersed, advised him to withdraw his few remaining men, replenish ammunition and reassemble his command. As Hays and a few Georgians with him, a mere handful, fell back through Hood's advancing line, then moving obliquely to the East Woods, fire was opened to the front and left, at the same time it was observed that the left flank of the division was exposed to a flank attack from a body of men on the high ground near the Hagerstown road, upon which Hood ordered Wofford's Brigade, which had advanced about 150 yards, after reaching the clover field, to move obliquely to the left, Law's Brigade still continuing its course to the northeast, which would have carried it into the East Woods, left at the southeast corner of the corn, but,

---

[5] Carman notes: One of the most difficult things to determine in considering a great battle, is the hour that particular events took place, and the length of time troops were engaged. No two or more men will agree upon such points. Those of undoubted and equal courage, will contend for largely varying periods. This difficulty confronts us at every step and upon nearly every page of the official reports of Antietam, but a close analysis of the movements up to this period of action, leads to the conclusion that it was 7 a.m. when Hood crossed the Hagerstown road, at the church, and it was at this time that Colquitt's Brigade was seen moving from the Sunken Road. (Statement to the writer of Capt. Robbins, 4th Alabama, and Capt. Nisbet of 21st Georgia.)

Hood's point of view as they swept north toward the Cornfield, taken where the 6th North Carolina would have swept past the Smoketown Road. *Author's collection.*

a moment after the order was given to Wofford and promptly conveyed to his left regiment only, Law was ordered to change direction to the left to strike the southeast corner of the cornfield and a Union line south of it— the 90th Pennsylvania—which, in addition to a severe artillery fire, was rapidly firing and doing him much harm.

With three regiments of his brigade on open ground, the 4th Alabama following in the woods on his right, and the 1st Texas of Wofford's brigade on his left, Law, changing direction a little to the left, marched over ground covered with dead and wounded Georgians and, still under artillery fire, by which many men were struck down, made directly for the 90th Pennsylvania, firing as he advanced and threatening both flanks of the regiment, particularly its left. The fire of four regiments in front and on left flank and gradually reaching the right flank, also, was more than the 90th Pennsylvania could stand; everything on its left and immediate right, except Thompson's Battery, had gone, the enemy was about to pass both its flanks, and, after a stand in which it had lost nearly one half its men, having now only 100 in the ranks, it fell back slowly to the East Woods, the color bearer walking backwards and the men turning and firing, until it entered the woods, when it pushed hurriedly through them, closely followed to their farther edge by the 4th Alabama, and thence to the Poffenberger spring, where it halted and reformed.

Upon the retreat of the 90th Pennsylvania Law advanced a short distance until near the corn and momentarily halted, until the regiments on the left could be obliqued and the 4th Alabama came up through the woods on the right. In reaching the clover field, as it came out of the woods at the church, the 4th Alabama was crowded out of the field and into the Smoketown road, down which it went by the right flank, Trimble's men retiring as it went forward and the 26th and 94th New York and 88th Pennsylvania falling back as it approached the East Woods. When it reached the point where the road struck a southwest projection of the woods it came under a scattering fire from the woods, by which Captain Scruggs was wounded, and the command of the regiment passed to Captain W. M. Robbins.

Here what was left of the 21st Georgia, under command of Captain J. C. Nisbet, that had not retired with its brigade, came over the field from the right and desired to continue in action, and Robbins advised it to fall in on his right. All this occurred while pulling down the fence on the left of the road and, with scarce a minute's delay, the 4th Alabama went forward into line and pushed into the woods, the Georgians on its right, all moving northerly, yelling and firing at the 90th Pennsylvania as it went out of the woods, and then turning upon the 6th Pennsylvania Reserves, which, but a few minutes before, had been moved from its earlier position in the woods near the northeast corner of the corn, farther south in the woods and quite near where the Smoketown road emerges from them. The regiment had

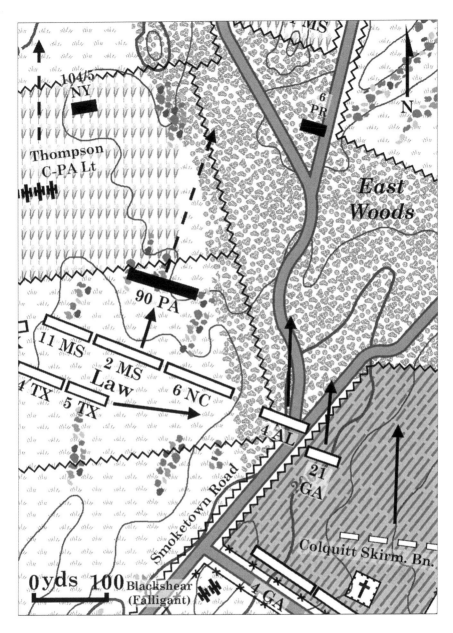

Law's Brigade moves north to engage the 90th Pennsylvania. The 5th Texas, drifting from Wofford's Brigade, and the 21st Georgia join in the advance. Colquitt's skirmish battalion falls in with the 4th Alabama and 5th Texas.

been more or less severely engaged from the beginning of the battle, its ammunition was well nigh exhausted and Robbins' attack, reinforced by the fire of the right of Law's Brigade in the open ground, forced it out of the woods northerly, to the Poffenberger woods, bordering the Smoketown road. This part of the East Woods being cleared, Robbins rested his left on the fence separating the cornfield and the woods, and about at the southeast corner of the corn, where, sheltered by trees and rocks, he kept up a skirmish fire to the front and obliquely to the left, into the northeast corner of the corn and the woods adjacent. Soon after taking position the 5th Texas came into the woods and formed on the right of the Georgians, and all remained there, a staunch body on the Confederate right, until the advance of Greene's Division, Twelfth Corps, swept the Confederate forces from the East Woods and fields adjoining to the west side of the Hagerstown road.

Thompson's Battery held on until it was seen that the 90th Pennsylvania was moving out and that Hood's men were nearing the cornfield, when, its men and horses falling fast, Thompson gave the order to withdraw. It went back, followed by a shower of bullets, and gained the high ground east of D. R. Miller's from which it had advanced into the corn, and the moment it was halted 18 horses fell dead and the guns were temporarily abandoned, until teams could be obtained to haul them off. The battery had 11 men wounded, and lost 23 horses killed and many wounded. As it went back Ransom's Battery was going into position.

Ricketts' Division with the exception of a few men of Duryee's Brigade, who had rallied in the northeast part of the cornfield and north part of the East Woods, had retired from the front to the open fields and woods beyond, the 90th Pennsylvania and Thompson's Battery being the last to go—but Matthews' still held on in the grass field north of the corn. The 6th Pennsylvania Reserves, the last of Seymour's Brigade, save a few men who still clung to the north part of the woods, had just been pushed back by the right of Law's Brigade.

Meade's two brigades—Magilton and Anderson—with Ransom's Battery (C, 5th U. S.), were now in position to meet the farthest advance of Hood's Division, and on their right Stewart's guns with Patrick's Brigade and the 19th Indiana and 7th Wisconsin, with the remains of the 2nd and 6th Wisconsin and Phelps' men are still in the fight.

Soon after Doubleday became engaged along the Hagerstown road and Ricketts in the East Woods and south of the corn, Hooker ordered Meade forward in the center with the brigades of Magilton and Anderson and Ransom's Battery. Magilton who was in the east part of the North Woods, closed in to the right on Anderson; Ransom moved from his position east of the Poffenberger barn, and all went out of the North Woods and halted on their south edge, the two brigades in column of battalion in mass, the

Brigadier General (later Major General) George G. Meade.
Library of Congress.

battery on the left of the infantry. A short halt and all went forward, came under a scattering fire from the cornfield and from some of S. D. Lee's guns, which created some confusion in the ranks of Magilton's Brigade, and, passing to the left of Miller's orchard, the two brigades obliqued to the right and were massed in the shallow basin extending up to the Hagerstown road, the ground over which Gibbon, Phelps and Patrick had moved to the attack. Meade led the infantry and Hooker directed the movements of the battery, which he put in position on the ground vacated by Stewart's two guns, near Miller's orchard. At this time Thompson's Battery came out of the corn and Hooker ordered Ransom to open fire upon Hood.

While advancing from the North Woods the 10th Pennsylvania Reserves was detached from Anderson's Brigade and sent beyond the Hagerstown road to protect Patrick's flank, who was in the West Woods in support of the 19th Indiana and 7th Wisconsin, with the 80th New York in support of Stewart's two guns, Campbell with the other four guns being on the way to join him.

Meade thus reports his movement from the North Woods to the front:

> Ransom's Battery was advanced into the open ground between the two advancing columns [Doubleday and Ricketts] and played with great effect on the enemy's infantry and batteries. The brigades of Anderson and Magilton on reaching the cornfield were massed in a ravine extending up to the pike. Soon after forming, I saw that the enemy were driving our men from the cornfield. I immediately deployed both brigades and formed line of battle along the fence bordering the cornfield, for the purpose of covering the withdrawal of our people and resisting the further advance of the enemy. Just as this line of battle was formed I received an order from the general commanding the corps to detach a brigade to reinforce our troops in the woods on the left. I directed Magilton to move in that direction.

Magilton's brigade was composed of the 3rd, 4th, 7th and 8th Pennsylvania Reserves; the 7th was on the right, 3rd and 4th in the center, and the 8th on the left. Immediately upon receipt of Meade's order, the brigade started by the left flank, moving parallel and quite close to the north fence of the cornfield, and quickly came under a terrific fire from the cornfield, from Law's advancing brigade and probably from the 1st Texas, also.

We left Law at a temporary halt near the south edge of the corn. Before he reached this point the 1st Texas, which had been moving on his immediate left, the 4th and 5th Texas having been crowded out of line, was ordered to oblique to the left, following the 18th Georgia and the Hampton Legion; at the moment of halting, the 4th Texas, which had by some means

Looking south from the location of Ransom's Battery B, 5th United States. The northern fence of the Cornfield is in the center. Barely visible in the far center background, just to the left of the trees, is the modern Visitor's Center, the location of Col. S. D. Lee's artillery battalion. *Author's collection.*

changed position with the 5th, came up in rear of the 11th Mississippi and laid down, and the 5th Texas was formed in rear of the 1st and was about to follow it into the cornfield, when Hood rode up and, remarking that the 1st Texas could attend to the business in hand at that point, ordered the 5th to move to the right into the East Woods, where, as we have seen, it formed on the right of the 4th Alabama and the Georgians, and the 4th Texas was ordered to the left to support the 18th Georgia and the Hampton Legion, then engaged near the Hagerstown road with Stewart's guns and the 80th New York, but, before the 4th Texas had gotten to its feet Law was in motion and two companies of the Texans, misunderstanding orders, went with him.

Law's temporary halt near the south edge of the corn was by Hood's order, and was of brief duration, not to exceed five minutes, probably not more than two or three minutes, only sufficient time to allow Robbins with the 4th Alabama to come up on the right and the 1st Texas to gain a little ground to the left to form closer connection with the two regiments of Wofford near the Hagerstown road. At the end of this time the entire division advanced and the fighting became desperate from the East Woods on the right to the Hagerstown road on the left. As Hood ordered the general advance a staff officer came from Jackson to inquire as to the situation, to which Hood gave answer: "Tell General Jackson unless I get reinforcements I must be forced back, but I am going on while I can."

We first follow the advance on the right. Law did not cease firing when he came to his brief halt and as he swept into the corn he encountered the fire of about 100 men of the 104th and 105th New York and some of other organizations, but this did not materially check the advance, the Union men were soon driven out and, as Law's men neared the north fence of the corn, Matthews double shotted his guns with canister and poured it into them, thinning the ranks most terribly. Still they did not halt; as they approached the fence Magilton's Brigade was moving by the left flank across their front, and upon it they opened fire, breaking the 3rd and 4th Pennsylvania Reserves, who retreated in some disorder, but the 8th Reserves, though losing heavily, kept on and gained the cover of the woods, where, with only 50 men, it turned and opened effectively upon Law's men as they reached the north fence of the corn; Ransom was training his guns upon them and Matthews, giving them one more round of canister, as some of them came over the fence, abandoned his guns, and Reynolds' New York battery, went to the rear without being able to fire a shot. The 6th North Carolina, upon reaching the fence, was so much exhausted and reduced in numbers that its aggressive force was gone; it held ground and returned the fire of the 8th Reserves, in which it was assisted by Robbins in the East Woods. Those who crossed the fence were of the 2nd and 11th Mississippi; as they did so, they caught sight of the 7th Reserves upon their left, which had been cut

This is the view the 11th Mississippi would have had of the Union position at the northern fence of the Cornfield. The modern cannon display (actually for Thompson's Battery C, Pennsylvania Light Artillery) marks the approximate position of Ransom's Battery C, 5th United States. *Author's collection.*

off in the act of following the 3rd and 4th Reserves, and they immediately turned to the left and opened fire upon it. The Pennsylvanians had just begun their flank movement to the left, when they saw the Mississippians coming over the fence, upon which they came into line nearly perpendicular to the fence and with about 150 men returned the fire which was poured into them. It was going hard with the Pennsylvanians, nearly one half were killed or wounded, when the enemy saw a large regiment of the Twelfth Corps approaching, and fell back into the cornfield, the 7th Reserves retiring to the ravine near the Hagerstown road.

The Mississippians went over the fence into open ground without orders either from brigade or regimental commanders. Colonel Stone, 2nd Mississippi, observing that the right of the line had passed much beyond the 4th Alabama, which was still fighting in the woods and unable to advance, was unwilling to hazard the safety of his command by going beyond the corn and over the open ground to the woods on the right, where the 8th Reserves was holding on; and the 11th Mississippi, on the left, was deterred from going forward because of the forbidding presence of Ransom's Battery, which, but 150 yards on its left front, was turning its guns upon it, so, these two regiments, as well as the 6th North Carolina, were ordered to halt at the north fence of the cornfield, but, as we have seen, some of them would not be restrained and went over the fence, driving Matthews from his guns and the 7th Reserves back to near the Hagerstown road. When these impulsive men fell back, so that their comrades could open fire, all retired a few feet from the fence and to the right, where the lay of the ground gave more protection and, while the 6th North Carolina was engaging the 8th Pennsylvania Reserves and some of the 3rd and 4th, who had now rallied on it, the two Mississippi regiments, with the 1st Texas on their left, paid particular attention to Ransom's guns and with such effect that they were temporarily silenced. Ransom says the musket balls cut several spokes from the wheels of his gun carriages. They also delivered a left oblique fire upon the heads and shoulders of Anderson's men, who were lying along the fence, nearer the Hagerstown road, engaged with Wofford, and upon the advance of the Twelfth Corps, then appearing on the high ground beyond. Particular attention was paid to a Union officer on a white horse, who was riding quietly about, sometimes in front of the line and sometimes in rear and an order was passed down the line of the 11th Mississippi: "Shoot the man on the white horse." Many shots were aimed at him but when last seen by the Mississippians he and his horse were apparently untouched.

The man on the white horse was Hooker, who had risen early and mounted his favorite white horse. He was dressed with scrupulous care as usual, as though for a ceremonial parade, and his striking figure was indeed a good mark for the Mississippi riflemen. He was exceedingly active that

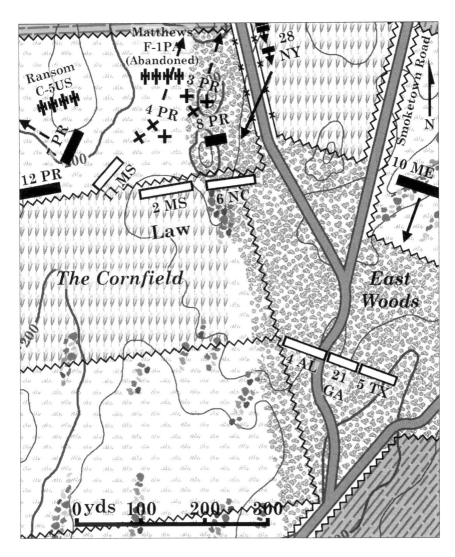

Law's Brigade reaches the north fence of the Cornfield and drives away much of Magilton's Pennsylvania Reserve brigade. The 10th Maine from the Twelfth Corps arrives and engages the 4th Alabama, 21st Georgia, and 5th Texas in the East Woods.

morning, giving personal direction to the movement of every regiment, brigade, and division, and the posting of every battery, and at all times was at the extreme front under fire. He met the brigades of Doubleday's Division as they emerged from the North Woods and gave orders in person for their deployment and advance; he rallied parts of Duryée's Brigade as they were falling back under the orders of the brigade commander; he ordered Hartsuff forward; he rode with Ransom's Battery, impetuously hastening it into position as Hood's men were seen coming through the corn; rallied the 3rd and 4th Pennsylvania Reserves, when their ranks were broken by Law's Brigade, and was now seen by the Mississippians directing the advance of the Twelfth Corps into action. He was everywhere present and everywhere his presence was an inspiration.

As Law was now threatened in front and on the right, by the advance of Crawford's Brigade of the Twelfth Corps, he gave orders to retreat. He makes this report:

> The...regiments of my command continued steadily to advance in the open ground, driving the enemy in confusion from and beyond his guns. So far we had been entirely successful and everything promised a decisive victory. It is true that strong support was needed to follow up our success, but this I expected every moment. At this stage of the battle, a powerful Federal force (ten times our number) of fresh troops were thrown in our front. Our losses up to this time had been very heavy; the troops now confronting the enemy were insufficient to cover properly one-fourth of the line of battle; our ammunition was expended; the men had been fighting long and desperately, and were exhausted from want of food and rest. Still, they held this ground, many of them using such ammunition as they could obtain from the bodies of our own men and the enemy's dead and wounded. It was evident that this state of affairs could not long continue. No support was at hand. To remain stationary or advance without it would have caused a useless butchery, and I adopted the only alternative—that of falling back to the wood from which I had first advanced.

General Meade makes this report of the action at the time Law retired:

> Anderson's Brigade still held the fence on the right, but the gap made by the withdrawal of Magilton was soon filled by the enemy, whose infantry advanced boldly through the cornfield to the woods. Seeing this I rode up to Ransom's Battery and directed his guns on their advancing columns, which fire, together with the arrival of Magilton's Brigade... drove the enemy back, who, as they retreated were enfiladed

View of the northern Cornfield fence looking east. This is what the 7th Pennsylvania Reserves or the left units of Anderson's brigade would have seen. The 11th Mississippi would have crossed the fence in the center. *Author's collection.*

by Anderson, who eventually regained the crest of the ridge in the cornfield.

Law's three regiments went back rapidly under a heavy fire of infantry and artillery and rallied for a moment on the south edge of the corn, where it was discovered that most of its officers had been killed and wounded, over half of the men gone and the colors of the 11th Mississippi left behind, in the corn, the color bearers having been killed. The stricken regiments did not long halt, but went back to the rear of the Dunker Church. Robbins with the 4th Alabama and the 5th Texas and Georgians remained in the East Woods. Of the three regiments that advanced through the cornfield more than one half were killed and wounded; nearly all the officers, including every field officer, were killed and wounded; in some companies every man was struck; the 2nd Mississippi lost all of its field officers, and nearly every company commander and came out of action under a second lieutenant. In the 11th Mississippi but one officer escaped unhurt, and it and the 6th North Carolina went out in charge of junior captains.

While Law was thus most deadly engaged on the right Wofford was as bloodily engaged on the left, on and near the Hagerstown road. We take up our narrative here where we left Gibbon's and Phelps' men pressing the defeat of Starke and their sudden check by the appearance of Hood's Division swarming out of the woods at the church and opening fire on them. When Hood gave the order, soon after gaining the open field, for Wofford to oblique to the left, the Hampton Legion and 18th Georgia were immediately set in motion in that direction, but the rest of the brigade did not receive the order and the movement became a disjointed one. The Hampton Legion and 18th Georgia moved obliquely to the open ground bordering the Hagerstown road, the left of the Legion resting on the crest near the road, with the 18th Georgia on its right, and became engaged with the 2nd and 6th Wisconsin and Phelps' men as they retired. Seeing the two regiments moving slowly forward, but rapidly firing, Wofford rode to them to urge a quicker pace, when he saw two full regiments in their front; one of these was the 14th Brooklyn, with others of Phelps' Brigade rallied on it, the other was the 2nd Wisconsin. The Hampton Legion and the 18th Georgia advanced, under a heavy fire of musketry in front and artillery on the right, three color bearers of the Legion being shot down in quick succession, when the colors were seized and carried by Major J. H. Dingle, who was killed when nearing the cornfield.

A little before this the 4th Texas had been ordered by Hood to move from the rear of the 11th Mississippi to the left, until its left rested on the crest of the high ground, in advance, near the road. Moving on the double quick the indicated position was occupied and then it was ordered by Hood

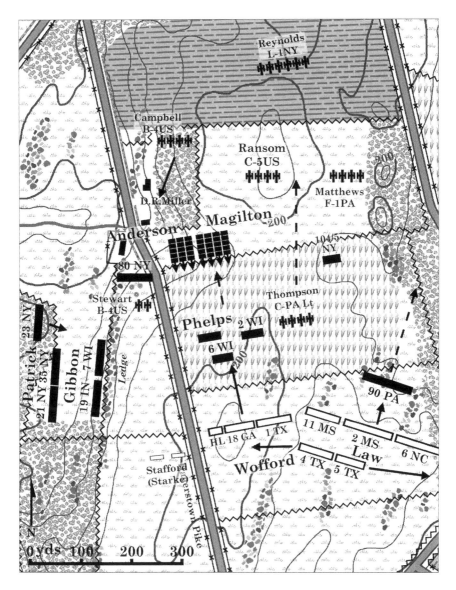

Wofford's Brigade advances into the Cornfield, driving back Gibbon.
Anderson and Magilton from Meade's Pennsylvania Reserves arrive at the
northern fence of the Cornfield. Thompson's Battery C, Pennsylvania Light
is abandoned near Ransom's Battery C, 5th United States, but is left off
subsequent maps to avoid clutter.

directly up the rise of ground on the left of the 18th Georgia and the Legion, then slowly advancing. Wofford, meanwhile, had seen that those two regiments were in danger of being cut off by a force threatening their left and ordered the 1st Texas, which had advanced on Law's immediate left to move by the left flank to their relief, which it did in a rapid and gallant manner, just as the Union forces east of the road were driven back into the corn by the 18th Georgia and Hampton Legion, and by a part of Starke's line, which had rallied and moved up the road and along the fence on the west side of it, and opened fire into the cornfield and threatened Stewart's guns. The two regiments were now checked by a terrible fire from Stewart's guns and the supporting infantry across the road; and the 1st Texas, as it came up on their right by the left flank, fronted and charged into the cornfield in pursuit of the New York and Wisconsin men, who were quickly driven out of the corn, and over Anderson's Brigade, the colors of the 2nd Wisconsin through the ranks of the 11th Pennsylvania Reserves, those of the 14th Brooklyn through the 9th Pennsylvania Reserves, and were rallied in Anderson's rear, in the shallow basin or ravine between the cornfield and Miller's orchard.

The 1st Texas had been ordered to halt at the south edge of the corn, that a proper alignment of the brigade could be made, but failed to get or heed the order and, as Hood later explained: "slipped the bridle and got away from the command," and could not be restrained until it had pushed far into the cornfield, its colors about 150 yards from the Hagerstown road. Here its reception was a warm one. Ransom's battery opened upon it, as it reached the highest ground in the corn, and when it approached to within 30 yards of the north fence of the corn it was met by a deadly fire of Anderson's Brigade which, as we have seen, Meade, but a few minutes before, had deployed along the fence; the 9th Pennsylvania Reserves, Captain Samuel B. Dick, on the right, its right on and in the Hagerstown road, the 11th Reserves, Lieutenant-Colonel Samuel M. Jackson, on the left of the 9th, and the 12th Reserves, Captain Richard Gustin, on the left of the 11th. The regiments had not been long in this position when the New York and Wisconsin men began to come out of the corn in some confusion and reporting that the enemy was close behind them. The order was now passed along the line to fire as soon as all the Union men had come in, the Pennsylvanians steadied their guns on the lower rails of the fence, and when the legs of the Texans were seen about 30 yards from the fence, in front of the 11th Reserves, fire was opened by it and the 12th Reserves; the 9th followed with a volley obliquely to the left and, at the same time, Gibbon's men, beyond the Hagerstown road, opened full upon its flank and rear, and the regiment was laid low, a squad only remained to fall back, leaving their colors on the field, eight of their color bearers being shot down in quick

Colonel Samuel M. Jackson, 11th Pennsylvania Reserves
Library of Congress

succession. Of the 226 officers and men taken into action, 170 were killed or wounded and 12 missing, or 80 53/100 per cent of the number engaged.

We [Carman] have before us a letter of Lieut. Col. Work, written February 13, 1891, in which he says:

> The morning reports, by company commanders, on the morning of the 16th, showed (including field officers, Major Dale, Adjutant Shropshire and myself) a total regimental strength of 226. After dark on the evening of the 16th, two men from each of the twelve companies of the regiment were detailed and sent to the rear for the purpose of roasting green corn as food for the regiment. Less than half of them had rejoined the regiment, when, just after day dawn [sic], on the 17th, we were ordered forward—and by this means, we went into action with about 15 men less than 226.

With this deduction the regiment had 211 in action and its loss of 182 was 86 1/4 per cent.

The loss in each of the twelve companies, shows 50 killed, 132 wounded, 4 missing, an aggregate of 186. In two companies every officer and man were killed or wounded. Of 26 officers 7 were killed and 11 wounded. Conceding the accuracy of Col. Work's statement that the regiment had 211 in action, its loss was 23 69/100 per cent killed, 86 1/4 per cent killed and wounded, and 88 15/100 per cent in killed, wounded and missing.

The color lost was the "Lone Star" flag made from the wedding dress of Mrs. L. T. Wigfall, whose husband, formerly Senator Wigfall, had been colonel of the 1st Texas. Its loss was not discovered until the regiment was moving out of the corn and when it was too late to hunt for it as Patrick's men were pressing its flanks and Anderson's came within a few yards of its rear. Work reports that he was:

> well convinced that had the 18th Georgia and Hampton Legion not met with the most obstinate and stubborn resistance from a superior force to their left, they would have supported me promptly and effectively upon my left, and that that portion of the enemy's force in our front would have been routed, the tide of battle there turned, and the day been ours.

The 18th Georgia and the Hampton Legion could not go forward because they were checked by the fire of Stewart's guns and the supporting infantry. We left Stewart throwing spherical case at Starke's retreating men. When he saw Hood moving toward the cornfield he turned his guns upon him and those swarming up the road and in the field, close to the fence, in which were his guns, and threw canister as rapidly as his men could handle

12-pdr Napoleon smoothbore cannon. A popular weapon used by both sides including Ransom's Battery C, 5th United States, and Campbell's Battery B, 4th United States. *Author's collection.*

it. But still the Confederates pressed on, and, under cover of the fences and the corn, some crept close to his guns, picking off the gunners so rapidly that in less than ten minutes from the time he had taken position 14 of his men were killed and wounded, and the two guns were temporarily silenced, but not before they had done terrible execution in the ranks of the 18th Georgia and Hampton Legion. Stewart's horse was killed and, in falling, threw him; as soon as he could rise he ran back to the stacks, behind which the caissons had been left, and ordered the drivers to accompany him to the front and take the places of the dead and wounded cannoneers. By the time he had returned with these to the guns Captain Campbell, commanding the battery, coming at a gallop down the road from the Miller field, brought the other four guns into battery on the left of Stewart's section and began firing canister into the cornfield and the field south of it, where the Confederates were seen near the east fence of the road. In a very short time Campbell was severely wounded, and the command fell to Stewart. General Gibbon, seeing the danger threatening and observing the gunner of the left piece fall, ran into the battery and acted as gunner. What was left of Phelps' Brigade and the 2nd and 6th Wisconsin, not over 150 men, in all, were brought across the road, from where they had rallied when driven from the cornfield, and, merging with the 80th New York, drew close to the guns: those on the left opened fire into the cornfield, those on the right, with bayonets fixed, lying down behind the guns. In the full uniform of a general officer, his face begrimed by powder, and perspiration running down his cheeks, Gibbon was still serving the gun of his old battery, yet almost despairing of saving them. Double charges of canister were thrown into the corner of the cornfield, the aim was low, the stones and dirt on the road were plowed up, the fence rails were splintered and thrown into the air, and as smoke and dust cleared away, groups of the enemy were seen running to the rear, and, looking to the right, there was seen a Union line sweeping across the front of the guns up the road. It was a few minutes before this that the 4th Texas, Lieutenant Colonel B. F. Carter, which had come from the right and halted at the brow of the ridge, moved up and received a scattering fire from the ledge 150 yards beyond the road. Carter wheeled his regiment to the left, drew up along the road fence and replied to the fire from the ledge; about 50 men, catching sight of a Confederate flag in possession of Gibbon's men, beyond the road, charged to retake it, but were checked before they had crossed the second fence and lay down on the west side of the road, under shelter of the fence and a ditch on that side. It was at this time that the officers of the Hampton Legion and 18th Georgia saw that Law's men and the 1st Texas were falling back on their right and that on their left, not 200 yards distant, a Union line covered their entire flank, advancing in an oblique direction, threatening to cut them off,

Campbell's Battery B, 4th United States position west of the Hagerstown Turnpike. The 1st Texas outflanked this position in its charge through the Cornfield and reached to about the tree in the right background. *Author's collection.*

when they gave the order to fall back, simultaneously with Gibbon's last shot that sent the fence rails flying into the air.

The five small regiments in this advancing line were the 19th Indiana, 7th Wisconsin, 21st, 23rd, and 35th New York. When the left of the skirmish line of the 19th Indiana, on the higher ground in the West Woods, saw the advance of Hood's Division, passing their flank, they reported the fact to Lieutenant Colonel Bachman, who with the regiment, was still in the west woods, on much lower ground, and the information was conveyed to the 7th Wisconsin and Patrick's Brigade. Bachman at once called in the skirmishers from his right and front, and with his regiment and the 7th Wisconsin, changed front to the left, moved out of the woods to the ledge and opened fire on the Confederates lying in the road and beyond it, and another line along the fence in an open field about 100 yards distant, driving the latter line back, but the 4th Texas still held ground. Bachman, yielding to the urgent appeals of the men, gave the order to charge and hat in hand, with drawn sword, led them on the "double quick" all cheering as they advanced. At the same time the 7th Wisconsin sprang over the rock ledge and went forward on the left of the 19th Indiana, closely followed by Patrick's three regiments. It was the sight of these advancing regiments that caused the retreat of the Hampton Legion and the 18th Georgia. The 4th Texas, in danger of being cut off by the 19th Indiana, started to move off by the left flank, before the 19th Indiana could intercept it, but had moved only a few feet along the fence, when its commander, Carter, saw that the regiment was so much exposed and that it could not escape in that direction that he halted, opened fire on the 7th Wisconsin, which had nearly reached the road, repulsed it, and immediately fell back under the hill, to reform and was ordered by Hood to move to the Dunker Church. The 19th Indiana was temporarily checked, but finally went on, crossed the road and followed the Confederates to the brow of the ridge, over which was seen a strong force of infantry (Ripley's Brigade) which opened fire, Bachman was mortally wounded, and Dudley succeeded to the command. As soon as Bachman could be carried to the rear, the regiment fell back to the road and rallied in it; on its left were Patrick's regiments—the 21st, 23rd, and 35th New York.

When the 19th Indiana and 7th Wisconsin changed front to the left, to strike Hood's flank, Patrick was in the north part of the West Woods in support to them. He also changed front and moved obliquely to the left with the 21st and 35th New York to the rock ledge, where he was quickly joined by the 23rd New York, which, early in the action, had been sent to the right, but now had been relieved by the 10th Pennsylvania Reserves. The 21st and 35th New York reached the ledge just as the 7th Wisconsin went over it and the 19th Indiana farther to the right was making its charge. As the Wisconsin men fell back from the hot fire of the 4th Texas, the 21st

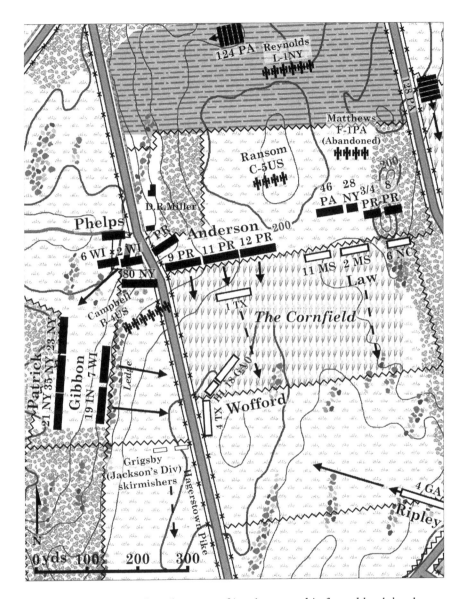

The 1st Texas reaches the apex of its charge and is forced back by the advance of Anderson's brigade. The arrival of Crawford's brigade from the Twelfth Corps prompts Law to retreat. The advance of the 19th Indiana, 7th Wisconsin, and Patrick force Wofford to fall back.

and 35th New York, closely supported by the 23rd, went forward through them, under a severe fire from the retreating Texans, and gained the road, the 21st going entirely across it and into the grass field beyond, but immediately fell back as the 19th Indiana on the right retreated and fell back to the road.

The venturesome Texans, who had been so eager to recapture the Confederate colors and who were in the road, near the southwest corner of the corn, were cut off by this quick advance of the Union line and, perceiving that the Union troops were already in the corn, started directly down the road in the direction of the church and were fired upon, some were killed and wounded, about 20 were captured, a few escaped by climbing the east fence of the road.

The repulse of Wofford gave Gibbon an opportunity to retire Stewart's guns. Forty battery men had been killed and wounded, 26 horses killed and 7 more disabled, and Stewart was ordered to resume the position held by his two guns earlier in the day, and the infantry supporting, much reduced, were ordered to the North Woods.

When the 19th Indiana and other regiments took position in the road no enemy was seen on their right, but they had been only a short time in the road when they were attacked in the flank and rear by Starke's men, who had been driven into the woods. The Union line presented such a tempting opportunity that portions of the Louisiana brigade were led by Colonel Stafford out of the woods and approaching, unobserved, to within 100 yards of the 19th Indiana gave it a rear and enfilade fire that caused it to fall back to the rock ledge, the movement being followed by Patrick, all his regiments in succession, changing front, engaging the enemy, finally driving them back to the woods and then taking position behind the ledge.

The 19th Indiana and 7th Wisconsin were moved to the rear near the West Woods and, after lying a short time under a severe artillery fire from Stuart's guns on their right, rejoined their brigade in the North Woods. Patrick held the ledge a few minutes longer, when, his ammunition being almost exhausted and his line attacked in flank and rear, he ordered his command to fall back to a low meadow near Miller's barn and behind a line of rock ledges at right angles to the road and about 15 rods from the West Woods, to await ammunition and reinforcements, where he remained, between the fire of opposing batteries, long enough to make coffee when we shall see him again engaged.

At the moment the Union line advanced to the road and saved Stewart's guns, Gibbon hastened across the road to Anderson's Brigade to have it go forward. Meade could not be found, being on the left of his line, and Gibbon ordered Anderson to push through the corn in pursuit of the Confederates, advising him that a part of his own brigade and Patrick's were still in and on the right of the road. Anderson's three regiments went

Looking uphill toward the Hagerstown Turnpike. This is the view the right of the 19th Indiana would have seen in this area as they advanced from the northern extension of the West Woods and rock ledge toward the Texas Brigade and pushed Grigsby's skirmishers away from this fence. *Author's collection.*

forward, the 1st Texas and others retiring before them, and the 9th Pennsylvania Reserves went clear through the corn to the open field where Wofford's men had been; the Union line, by this time, had been forced back from the road and Stewart's guns were going to the rear, but the regiment advanced about 75 yards beyond the corn, when it saw Ripley's Confederate brigade advancing across the low ground on its left front and immediately opened fire, to which Ripley's men promptly responded. Anderson rode back to get reinforcements, before he could return Captain Dick, commanding the regiment, learned that the 11th Pennsylvania Reserves, on his left, had fallen back, there was no support on his right, his men were falling fast, and he was obliged to fall back to the position from which he had advanced. The 11th and 12th Reserves, on the left of the 9th, advanced about half way through the corn, when they received such a severe fire that they were ordered to fall back, the 11th to the Hagerstown road and thence to the rear; the 12th through the corn to the shallow basin near the road, where it was joined by the 9th. Subsequently the 9th and 12th were relieved by the Twelfth Corps and Meade ordered them to join the division in support of the corps artillery.

While these three regiments were engaged in and near the cornfield, the 10th Pennsylvania Reserves, Lieutenant Colonel A. J. Warner, was in action on the extreme right, beyond the north part of the West Woods. As its brigade moved to the front this regiment was detached, and, crossing the road just before reaching Miller's house, went across the low meadow and relieved the 23rd New York, which rejoined its brigade in the advance to the road. Warner's skirmishers reported a Confederate brigade (Early's) moving behind a cornfield in the direction of the West Woods. Hooker was advised of the movement and the regiment pushed on to a fence running northwest from the corner of the woods; part of the regiment deployed as skirmishers, went into the cornfield to annoy Early and, if possible check and delay his movement. In these operations Warner was wounded and the command fell to Captain J. P. Smith. Early now detached the 13th Virginia to meet Warner's skirmishers; a battery was brought to bear on the regiment, which was drawn to the left, along the same fence, where, for the present, we leave it.

With the exception of Patrick's Brigade and the 10th Reserves, on its right, west of the Hagerstown road, and a few of Magilton's men in the north part of the East Woods, the infantry of Hooker's Corps was out of the fight, and Hood's Division, with the exception of the 4th Alabama and the 5th Texas, still in the East Woods, had withdrawn or was withdrawing to the woods at the Dunker Church, and Ripley's Brigade had become engaged with the Twelfth Corps.

Wofford had 854 men in action and lost 560 killed, wounded, and missing, or 65 1/2 per cent. Of the three regiments engaged at the road the

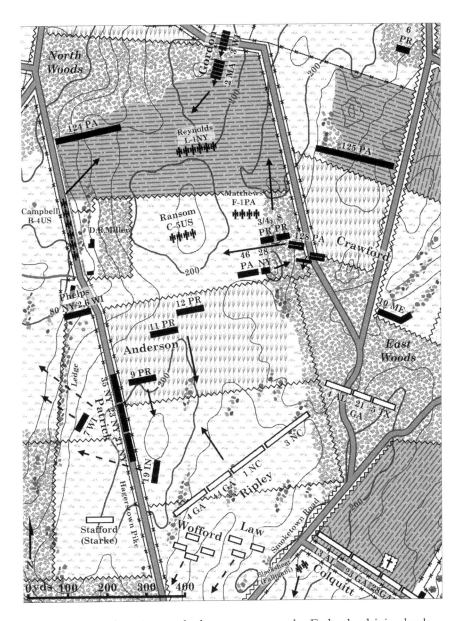

Ripley's Brigade arrives and advances to meet the Federals, driving back Patrick, and Gibbon. Remnants of Starke's Brigade under Colonel Stafford contribute by moving forward and flanking the units along the Hagerstown Turnpike.

Hampton Legion had 77 in action, and lost 55 killed and wounded, or 71 4/10 per cent; the 18th Georgia had 176 engaged, of whom 101 were killed, wounded or missing, or 57 per cent, and the 4th Texas, with 200 engaged, had 107 killed and wounded—53 1/2 per cent. The 1st Texas, as stated, had 211 in action, lost 182 killed and wounded, or 86 1/4 per cent. After giving the names of 12 officers killed, Wofford says: "They deserved a better fate than to have been, as they were, sacrificed for the want of proper support."

In *Advance and Retreat*, General Hood writes of his division:

> This most deadly contest raged till our last round of ammunition was expended. The 1st Texas regiment had lost in the cornfield fully two-thirds its number; and whole ranks of brave men, whose deeds were unnumbered, save in the hearts of loved ones at home, were mowed down in heaps to the right and left. Never before was I so continuously troubled with fear that my horse would further injure some wounded fellow soldier, lying helpless on the ground. Our right flank, during this short, but seemingly long, space of time, was toward the main line of the Federals, and, after several ineffectual efforts to procure reinforcements and our last shot had been fired, I ordered my troops back to the Dunker Church, for the same reason which compelled Lawton, Hays, and Trimble to retire.

In his official report Hood says:

> Fighting, as we were, at right angles with the general line of battle, and General Ripley's Brigade being the extreme left of General D. H. Hill's forces and continuing to hold their ground, caused the enemy to pour a heavy fire upon the rear and right flank of Colonel Law's brigade, rendering it necessary to move the division to the left and rear into the woods near the church.

The complaint made by Hood and his officers that they were not properly supported, is directed at both D. H. Hill and Ripley for not coming promptly to their assistance.

The events narrated in this chapter cover the period from daybreak to 7:30 a.m. Seymour's brigade and the artillery duel of both sides, opened the engagement at daybreak. Duryée's brigade went to the assistance of Seymour and became actively engaged with Lawton and Trimble at 6 a.m., and fell back a half hour later. Hartsuff, later supported by Christian, became engaged at 6:40 a.m. with Trimble, Lawton and Hays, the latter going to Lawton's assistance about 6:15 a.m. It was 6:30 a.m. when Gibbon, Phelps, and Patrick became engaged with Jackson's Division and the left of

The caption for this photo says "North Woods - near Dunker Church taken after the war" but it's possible the caption is mistaken and its actually the West Woods. Still, it shows the open nature of the woodlots on this section of the battlefield. *Library of Congress.*

Lawton, repulsing both; and 7:00 a.m. when Hood's Division crossed the Hagerstown road at the Dunker Church, relieved Lawton, Trimble and Hays, drove back the advance of Gibbon and Phelps, forced Hartsuff and Christian from the field, and was in turn checked and driven back by Gibbon, Patrick, Magilton and the First Corps artillery, aided by the timely appearance of the Twelfth Corps.

Chapter 16

The Battle on the Union Right and the Confederate Left (7:30 a.m. to 9 a.m.)

About two o'clock on the morning of the 17th the Twelfth Corps, Major General J. K. F. Mansfield commanding, after crossing the Antietam at the upper bridge, laid down to rest on the farms of Hoffman and Line, a short mile in the rear of Hooker's left. The men were informed that the enemy was in their immediate front and were ordered to rest on their arms, all of which was not conducive to sound sleep. The veteran commander spread his blanket in a fence corner, near Line's house, and had a fitful sleep. A few hours later he was brought back to Line's house to die.

Mansfield had assumed command of the corps on the 15th of September. He was 59 years of age, of venerable appearance, white haired, yet fresh and vigorous, with an open, intelligent countenance. He was an accomplished engineer officer, but had a limited experience in the handling of troops. His confidence in volunteer soldiers was not great, which may account for the fact that he insisted on leading his regiments into action closed in mass, contending against the remonstrance of his division commanders, that, if deployed, they would run away. His two days service with the corps had not impressed his immediate subordinates with great confidence in his military capacity, but had endeared himself to the men. He was oppressed with the responsibility of his command, and this and other circumstances impelled him to give personal attention to the movement of regiments and batteries, regardless of division and brigade commanders.

The Twelfth was a small corps, its whole effective force less than 7,500 men, strangers for the most part in the Army of the Potomac. The First Division had, little over a month previous, at Cedar Mountain, lost nearly all the field officers, and all the adjutants of one of its two brigades, and its ranks were so reduced that several of the old regiments numbered but little over 100 men. There were in this division five new regiments, not more than three weeks from home, which, in the rapid marches from Frederick, had been much reduced in numbers. The Second Division, 2,500 strong, had lost three general officers, wounded and prisoners, at Cedar Mountain, and its regiments were much reduced. The whole corps, excepting the new regiments, had been in continuous daily marches and there was neither time nor opportunity to restore the spirit and vigor to the command. And yet, under all these adverse circumstances, this corps, as we shall see, repulsed the Confederates who were exultingly driving Hooker from the field, drove them out of the East Woods, back over the open fields and beyond the Hagerstown road, and held these fields all day, without yielding an inch of ground, except the woods which it had seized around the Dunker Church.

It went into action without coffee or food, and after an almost sleepless night. At the first sound of cannon at daybreak of the "misty moisty morning," it was put in motion, crossed the Smoketown road, moved west a short distance, swung to the left and marched south in columns of battalions in mass; the first Division in advance, Crawford's Brigade leading, Gordon's following Crawford's, and Greene's Second Division bringing up the rear. From the moment of leaving the bivouac the column marched directly in the line of fire of Stephen D. Lee's guns. The advance was slow and cautious, and the haltings, by Mansfield's orders, very frequent, but not of sufficient time to allow the men to boil coffee. Regiments were detached to occupy woods on the flanks, brought back again and again detached. At 6:30 a.m., the head of column was halted near the middle of an open field west of and adjoining S. Poffenberger's woods, and Mansfield rode forward to survey the ground and consult with Hooker. At the time of the halt the old regiments of Crawford's Brigade—the 10th Maine, 28th New York, and 46th Pennsylvania—were on the right, and the new regiments—the 124th, 125th and 128th Pennsylvania—on the left. "It was the understanding that the latter three regiments should move to the front when wanted, and the old ones should follow at a proper distance in the rear, contributing, as it were, a reserve for the brigade."

When coming to a halt Williams observed that the regiments of his division had been moved up without deploying intervals; they were then under fire and liable at any moment to be called into action, as Hooker's Corps was melting away, much of it streaming to the rear, and, as Mansfield

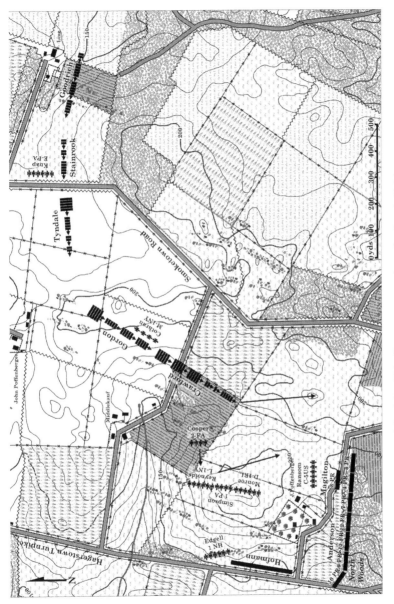

The Twelfth Corps approaches the battlefield.

rode to the front, Williams ordered the deployment of the brigade and Crawford proceeded to execute the order. When nearly completed Mansfield returned and ordered Crawford to suspend the deployment and again mass his command, although then exposed to artillery fire. Williams remonstrated, but Mansfield would not consent to a deployment in the open field, giving as a reason that if the new regiments were deployed in line they would run away, upon which Williams gathered the commanders of the old regiments under a large tree, and gave instructions as to deployment, Colonel Knipe, 46th Pennsylvania, being directed to double-quick in advance and cover the deployment of the new regiments, when the time came.

When Mansfield rode forward to report to Hooker, he was informed that the First Corps was hard pressed and that he would soon be called upon to relieve it. He had been back to his command but a few minutes and Williams had scarcely concluded his conference with the three regimental commanders, when Hooker's orders were received to deploy and advance. Directing Williams to lead the 124th and 125th Pennsylvania to the right, as far as the Hagerstown road, Mansfield advanced with the three old regiments and the 128th Pennsylvania, all still in columns of divisions. It was then about 7:15 a.m.

The original intention to move the three new regiments in advance, followed by the three old ones, was now departed from, and, in the advance, Knipe says: "The 10th Maine, which had been on the right of the 46th Pennsylvania, by some means for which I cannot account, got on the left of it, and both, with the 28th New York, in advance of the 124th, 125th and 128th Pennsylvania."

The departure from the original intention was due to Hooker's direction to Mansfield to form the three new regiments of Crawford's Brigade on the right, the right resting on the Hagerstown road; the old regiments to extend the line to the left, where the danger was now most imminent. Gordon was to deploy in rear of Crawford's new regiments as a support, and Greene's Division was to go in on the left of the old ones. It was in following these directions that Williams led the 124th and 125th Pennsylvania to the right, and Mansfield led the three old regiments and the 128th Pennsylvania to the front, intending to form the 128th Pennsylvania on the right, connecting with the 125th, with the old regiments on the left of the 128th. How the movement was executed and the result we shall now tell.

Before the general advance was made the 125th Pennsylvania had gone forward under the personal direction of Crawford, Colonel Higgins commanding the regiment, says:

> I was ordered by General Crawford to advance in close column, through some fields to a piece of woods, where there was a heavy

The Twelfth Corps approached the East Woods from this direction. In 1862 the corner of the North Woods was to the left, but the area in the right background was open except for the Samuel Poffenberger wood lot. *Author's collection.*

firing at that time going on. I was then ordered into the woods and then back again by General Crawford, then to throw out skirmishers and again advance into the woods until I reached the other side of the timber, and then deploy in line of battle and advance through the fields and there halt. At this place my command was exposed to a most terrific fire of musketry, shot and shell. I then fell back a few rods by order of General Crawford.

The regiment was in a slight depression in the ground, about 200 yards south of the S. Poffenberger woods, its left on the Smoketown road, its right extending westerly nearly to the J. Poffenberger lane. It was now ordered to advance through a 10 acre cornfield and occupy a knoll, along which ran a fence, separating the cornfield from the East Woods. A company of skirmishers passed through the corn and into the woods, closely followed by the regiment, and Robbins' men—Alabamians, Georgians, and Texans—were seen in the far part of the woods; before firing a shot the regiment and its skirmishers were recalled to the position from which they had been ordered forward. In its eccentric movements, exposed to "a terrific fire of musketry, shell and shot," as reported by Colonel Higgins, the loss was trifling, and the first man was killed after it had fallen back, by a shot from the East Woods. It had not fired a shot, but its movement in front and on the Confederate flank, steadied Meade's left, what little there was of it, enabled Magilton to partially reform his shattered brigade; held at bay Law's Confederate brigade, and finally, with the appearance of the 10th Maine, compelled Law to withdraw. Meanwhile the old regiments of the brigade came up, closely followed by the 128th Pennsylvania.

The advance of the old regiments was led by Mansfield in person, who rode with the 10th Maine on the left, which marched in column of divisions, closed in mass, and entered the 10 acre cornfield, east of the northern part of the East Woods, where it came under fire, while deploying, by which a few men were killed and wounded by a fire from the East Woods. As the regiment was about to return the fire, it was ordered to oblique to the left, the length of the regiment, and at once began the engagement with a regiment of the enemy. So far the official records; but Major Gould, in his *History of the 10th Maine,* says the regiment did not deploy in the 10 acre cornfield, but moved, still closed in mass, across the Smoketown road to a plowed field, where Mansfield left it. It was then 7:30 a.m. The regiment now deployed and, while doing so, saw a Confederate skirmish line—the 5th Texas—along the East Woods fence, and, under the fire of these Texans, which struck the 125th Pennsylvania, also, advanced and drove the Texans back into the woods, and, when reaching the fence,

The area east of the Smoketown Road shown here is where the 10th Maine deployed and moved south toward the East Woods. The area to the left and front would have been open grass and not trees like the modern photo. *Author's collection.*

saw before it the right of Hood's line—the 4th Alabama, the Georgians, and the 5th Texas in the edge of the woods. The right companies of the 10th Maine went over the fence and taking shelter of trees and logs opened fire upon the enemy. The right of the regiment rested on the Smoketown road, seven companies and a part of another behind or just over the fence, while two companies and part of a third were thrown back under cover of a rock ledge, to guard the flank, as there were no Union troops on its left, it being, at the time and until relieved the left of the corps line.

While the 10th Maine was thus getting into action on the left, the 28th New York and 46th Pennsylvania, moved through the small cornfield, into the East Woods and deployed, part in the woods and part in the open ground west of them, and opened fire on the Confederates directly south. The 28th New York carried about 60 men into action, and the 46th Pennsylvania had not to exceed 150 men. The deployment and advance of the two regiments and the near approach of the 125th Pennsylvania, relieved some of the Pennsylvania Reserves, who had held onto the woods, but some of them, mostly of the 8th Reserves, still remained. The firing was now severe on both sides, during which Knipe and the 46th Pennsylvania, were awaiting the arrival and deployment of the 128th Pennsylvania.

We consider Knipe's opponents. In the earlier part of Crawford's maneuvering, Hood's Division, save the 4th Alabama and 5th Texas, which, with some Georgians, remained in the East Woods, had retired, and Anderson's Brigade, of Meade's Division, charged through the cornfield on the heels of the 1st Texas and was obliged to fall back on the advance of Ripley's Brigade, with which, and the Confederates in the East Woods, Knipe was now contending. Ripley's Brigade was the left of D. H. Hill's Division and on the night of the 16th bivouacked in the field south and west of the Mumma house and about 125 to 150 yards from it, and in close support to Trimble's Brigade of Ewell's Division. The brigade was composed of the 1st and 3rd North Carolina, 4th and 44th Georgia, and numbered 1,349 officers and men; the largest regiment, 3rd North Carolina, had 547 officers and men, the smallest, 44th Georgia, 162 officers and men. In the brigade formation the 3rd North Carolina was on the right, and on its left, in order named, the 1st North Carolina, 44th and 4th Georgia. Ripley reports the early movements of the brigade:

> Early on the morning of the 17th the skirmishers of Colonel Walker's (Trimble's) Brigade of Jackson's corps, immediately on my left, became engaged, and the enemy from his batteries on the eastern bank of the Antietam opened a severe enfilading fire on the troops of my command, the position we had been ordered to occupy being in full view of nearly all his batteries. This fire inflicted serious loss before the troops were called into positive action, the men lying under it, without

The 10th Maine's position along the northern edge of the East Woods. The road in the center was not present in 1862, but was instead the location of the fence at the northern border of the woods. The cornfield to the right was the East Woods, the modern trees to the left were clear. *Author's collection.*

flinching, for over an hour, while the enemy plied his guns unceasingly. During the while, a set of farm buildings (Mumma's) in our front, were set on fire to prevent them being made use of by the enemy. At about 8 o'clock (7 a.m.) I received orders to close in to my left and advance. The troops sprang to their arms with alacrity and moved forward through the burning buildings, in our front, reformed on the other side, and opened a rapid fire upon the enemy (26th and 94th New York). While engaged in reforming the brigade, I received a shot in the neck, which disabled me, and the troops moved forward under command of Colonel Doles of the 4th Georgia regiment.

As soon as this line had been reformed Doles ordered an advance to the East Woods and the brigade had gone about half way when D. H. Hill rode up and word was passed down the line to change direction by the left flank, and, in column of 4's, it was led by Hill across the Smoketown road, just touching the projecting point of the East Woods, subjected to quite a brisk fire by which Major R. S. Smith, of the 4th Georgia, and others were killed. Upon clearing the road the leading regiment filed to the left in the direction of the Hagerstown road, followed in succession by the others, and all came into line facing nearly north, the right of the brigade resting near the southwest corner of the woods, as Hood's men were retiring in the direction of the church, but Robbins and his men were still fighting in the East Woods, his left very near the southeast corner of the corn. In front of Ripley's Brigade was the cornfield, beyond which, on an elevation, was seen a Union line of infantry, with Ransom's battery of Napoleon guns.

The Brigade was advanced, all in open ground, and the left and center of the line, the 4th and 44th Georgia and part of the 1st North Carolina, making a slight wheel to the left, engaged the 9th Pennsylvania on the high ground south of the corn and near the Hagerstown road, while the 3rd North Carolina and part of the 1st, moving straight ahead, the right along and near the East Woods, after some severe fighting, drove the 11th and 12th Pennsylvania Reserves from the corn, but did not enter it, as the left had been checked by the resistance of the 9th Reserves. When the 9th Reserves finally fell back the left of Ripley's line advanced to the high ground near the road and halted about 50 yards south of the cornfield fence. A part of the 1st North Carolina was now moved from the right center of the brigade to the left of the 4th Georgia and at nearly right angles to it, facing nearly west, to prevent a repetition of the Union tactics that had resulted so disastrously to the left of Wofford's Brigade. The skirmishers on the right now entered the cornfield and became engaged with the 28th New York and 46th Pennsylvania. The 128th Pennsylvania now came up.

When Mansfield had conducted the 10th Maine across the Smoketown road he rode back to the 128th Pennsylvania, led it on the double quick

The left of the 128th Pennsylvania near the East Woods had this view of the Cornfield and area to the south. *Author's collection.*

over the right of the 125th Pennsylvania and into the East Woods. The regiment was still in column of divisions. As it entered the woods men of the 3rd Reserves and others of Magilton's Brigade moved out. Upon reaching the woods Mansfield ordered Colonel Croasdale to deploy to the right through the woods and into the open ground west of them, his evident intention being then to bring the 28th New York and 46th Pennsylvania on the left of the 128th, and fill the interval between it and the 10th Maine, then carrying out Hooker's instructions to have the three old regiments on the left of the brigade. Croasdale gave the order to deploy and was instantly killed, Lieutenant Colonel Hammersly was severely wounded, and the command devolved upon Major Wanner. Meanwhile the regiment was endeavoring to deploy to the right but, instead of moving each company in succession, nearly the entire crowded to the right in some disorder. In this condition the right and center went through the woods into open ground, passing in rear of the 28th New York and 46th Pennsylvania, Mansfield remaining with the three left companies, which were deployed in the woods and on the knoll just east of them. About this time Mansfield was mortally wounded and carried from the field.[6]

The entire regiment was now under the fire of Ripley's and Robbins' men, was raw and inexperienced and, naturally, there was much confusion in the deployment of the right and center, which Wanner endeavored to complete, but which he found impossible. The greater part of the regiment had now gained the open ground and massed, in disorder, on the right of the 46th Pennsylvania, and some of the men had opened fire upon Ripley's men, in and beyond the cornfield. Colonel Knipe, commanding 46th Pennsylvania, says of the 128th: "At this moment seeing the uselessness of a regiment in that position I took the responsibility of getting it into line of battle the best way circumstances would admit. When this was accomplished, I returned to my own regiment and ordered an advance, which was gallantly made as far as the fence of the cornfield."

Major Wanner, at Knipe's suggestion, after he had succeeded in deploying his regiment, ordered a charge into the cornfield. The men started off in gallant style, cheering as they went down to the cornfield fence, the 46th Pennsylvania moving out of the way, into the woods. Upon arriving at the fence the regiment fired a few rounds into the corn and then charged nearly to the south edge, but was met by such a severe fire from Ripley's men, particularly from the 3rd and part of the 1st North Carolina, that it was compelled to fall back to the fence in some disorder, and, with

---

[6] "See note at end of this chapter." Note inserted by Carman discussing Mansfield's wounding and added at the end of the chapter as it was in the original manuscript.

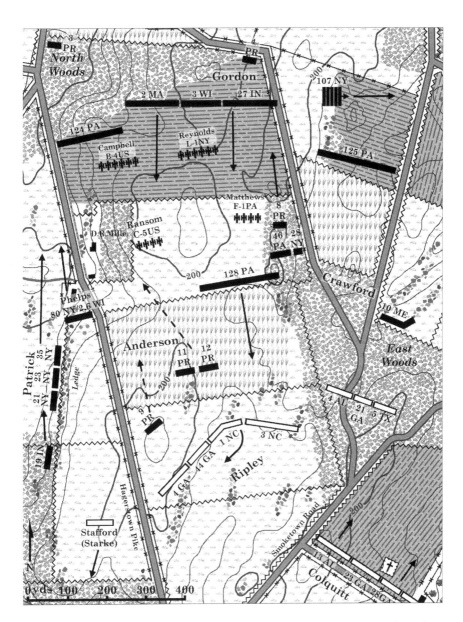

Anderson is driven from the Cornfield by fire from Ripley's Brigade. The 128th Pennsylvania moves into the corn, but is likewise driven back, pursued by Ripley's skirmishers.

the 46th Pennsylvania, was ordered into the woods, out of the line of fire of Gordon's Brigade, and then to the rear of the woods to reform.

The charge of the 128th Pennsylvania struck the 3rd North Carolina as it was changing front to the right to meet Greene's Division, seen in motion beyond the far edge of the East Woods and threatening its right. The regiment was thrown into some confusion, its colonel was wounded, many killed and wounded, and it gave ground, but was rallied and steadied by Lieutenant Colonel Thruston, and, driving back the Pennsylvanians, completed its change of front, which brought it entirely out of the corn, its left near the south edge of it, about 290 yards from the Hagerstown road. A strong line of brigade skirmishers re-entered the corn in pursuit of the Pennsylvanians, but the main line remained in the open ground south of the corn, exposed to the fire of Gordon's Brigade, Twelfth Corps.

We left General Williams moving to deploy the 124th Pennsylvania. He led it to the right and, passing through the eastern part of the North Woods, along the southern edge of which, starting one company after another by the flank, he formed the regiment in line, the right on the Hagerstown road, the left extending along the south edge of the woods. Williams ordered Colonel Hawley, as soon as the deployment should be completed and the other regiments of the brigade come up on the left, to move forward with them, but, after he had gone to attend the deployment of other regiments, it appears that Hooker, or some other general officer rode up and gave orders to hold the woods. It was after Williams had deployed the 124th Pennsylvania, and was in quest of the 125th, which he had ordered Crawford to deploy on the left of the 124th, that he found that the 125th had gone some distance to the left, and, at the same time, he heard that Mansfield had been mortally wounded. When this was reported to him he did not know that all the old regiments had gone to the front and then were in action, so he sent orders for their deployment and advance, and riding to the front, reported to Hooker, whom he found alone, in the plowed field, on the Miller farm, east of the Hagerstown road. Hooker's orders were to deploy in rear of the First Corps and relieve such portions of it as had not yet retired from the field.

While Williams was taking Hooker's instructions, Meade came from the left and Gibbon from the right, reporting their batteries in danger, and that they would be lost unless they had instant support and requested Williams to give it. He assured Hooker that Gordon's line of march would bring him to Meade's support, and that he would detach the rear brigade of Greene's Division to Gibbon's support, upon which Hooker, turning to Meade and Gibbon, remarked "Gentlemen, you must hold on until Williams' men get up," pointing at the same time to Gordon, then deploying south of the North Woods, and to Greene, hastening through the fields east of J. Poffenberger's. Greene was ordered to detach Goodrich's Brigade and send

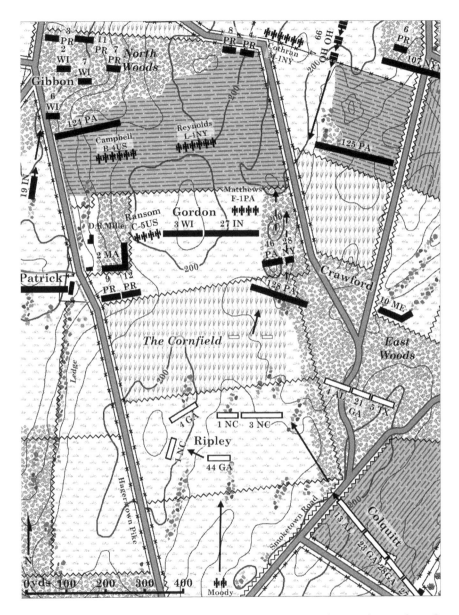

Ripley's skirmishers pursue the 128th Pennsylvania to the northern edge of the Cornfield. Gordon's brigade takes up position in the field to the north, and engage in a firefight with Ripley. Colquitt's Brigade moves north.

it across the Hagerstown road, to report to Gibbon or any general officer on that part of the field. At the same time an order was given the 124th Pennsylvania to push forward past D. R. Miller's, cross the Hagerstown road and into the woods beyond and hold the position as long as practicable, this on the supposition that Gibbon still held the right of the road, and not aware of the fact that Gibbon had already retired and that Patrick held the woods.

Having given his orders to Greene, Williams rode into the East Woods, where he saw that the 28th New York and 128th Pennsylvania had been roughly handled.

He informed Knipe that he was in command of the brigade, that Greene was to form on the left, and ordered him to look up his command, get it in order, and support Greene's right. At this time Gordon's old regiments— 2nd Massachusetts, 3rd Wisconsin, and 27th Indiana—were in line in the open field in good order.

Gordon's Brigade followed Crawford's from its bivouac on the Hoffman farm. Early in the movement the 13th New Jersey was detached and thrown into the edge of a piece of woods, to observe the right flank of the marching column, in the direction of the Hagerstown road, where, for the first time in its experience, its colonel instructed it how to form line of battle by deploying it along a fence, skirting the woods, much in the same manner as Williams had deployed the 124th Pennsylvania on the south border of the North Woods. After the long halt west of the Poffenberger woods Gordon was ordered to support a battery on the right, but, before reaching it, the order was counter-manded, and he was directed to move with all possible dispatch to the relief of the First Corps, then severely pressed and part of it giving way. Gordon moved double quick, passed through the eastern part of the North Woods, and formed line; the 2nd Massachusetts on the right, the 3rd Wisconsin in center, and the 27th Indiana on the left. The 107th New York, by order of Hooker, was thrown along the edge of the S. Poffenberger woods, on the left, to hold them and act as reserve. It was while thus deploying south of the North Woods that Williams called Hooker's attention to his advance. Gordon had expected to come up in rear of Crawford's new regiments, as a support to them, but he found nothing in his immediate front but fugitives and broken battalions of the First Corps, and, with the instinct of a true soldier, moved on to fill the gap in the line, and while moving one of Hooker's aides galloped up and requested him to hurry forward. "It was apparent," says Gordon, "from the steady approach of the rounds of musketry that the enemy were advancing. Their shouts of exultation could be distinctly heard as the line of my deployed battalions, sustained on the right by Crawford's Brigade (124th Pennsylvania only) and on the left by Greene's Division, both of our own corps, advanced boldly to the front."

Brigadier General George H. Gordon
Library of Congress.

The 3rd Wisconsin and the 27th Indiana advanced to the crest of a swell of ground immediately east of D. R. Miller's orchard and between it and the East Woods, the left of the 27th Indiana about 50 yards from the woods. Between the right of the 3rd Wisconsin and the orchard was Ransom's Battery of six guns, and on the line where the regiment halted were Thompson's abandoned guns. The 2nd Massachusetts, in its advance on the right, passed through Ransom's Battery, by which its movement was somewhat impeded, and going into the orchard was halted in its southeast corner some 75 yards in advance of the right of the 3rd Wisconsin, and was formed in a broken line, the left perpendicular and the right parallel to the line of the two other regiments, both wings of the regiment being along the orchard fences. In front of the right wing and about 50 yards distant, were two Union regiments, probably the 9th and 12th Pennsylvania Reserves, lying down obliquely to the Hagerstown road, in a depression of the ground. The 3rd Wisconsin was 150 yards from the cornfield fence, and the left of the 27th Indiana was 120 yards from the same fence. The strength of the three regiments was about 1,400 officers and men.

When the three regiments moved into position the 128th Pennsylvania was retreating out of the corn, pursued by the enemy. The corn was on lower ground, very heavy and served to screen the enemy, yet the colors and battle-flags clearly indicated their position and Colonel Colgrove, 27th Indiana, reports that he saw immediately beyond the corn, upon the open ground, at the distance of about 400 yards, three regiments in line of battle, and farther to the right, on a high ridge of ground, still another regiment in line diagonally to that of Gordon's Brigade. This accurately describes the position of Ripley's Brigade, which now opened a terrific fire upon Gordon, and which could not be immediately returned, for the 128th Pennsylvania had not yet come out of the corn, and there were still other Union men in front, about midway between the 27th Indiana and the cornfield fence. For more than five minutes the 3rd Wisconsin and 27th Indiana were compelled to stand a severe fire without replying, but, when the Pennsylvanians came out of the corn and Williams rode up and ordered them into the woods out of the way; Gordon's three regiments opened such a rapid and accurate fire that the pursuing enemy fell back and was soon reinforced by Colquitt's brigade.

On the night of the 16th Colquitt's Brigade bivouacked in the Sunken Road, near the Roulette lane. From right to left it was thus formed: 6th, 27th, 28th, and 23rd Georgia and 13th Alabama, which formation was preserved during the engagement. It numbered 1,320 officers and men. There was formed from this brigade a skirmish battalion of five companies, one from each regiment of the brigade, under command of Captain William Arnold of the 6th Georgia. The companies were formed from the right of each regiment and regularly drilled as skirmishers. Whenever skirmishing

Ripley's view of the battlefield. Gordon's Federals and Ransom's battery were arrayed on the high ground behind the Cornfield (the dark soybeans in this modern view). The two forces traded fire across this space, and Colquitt's Brigade deployed in the space here in front of Ripley. *Author's collection.*

was required this battalion was deployed, each company covering the front of its own regiment. When the main line became engaged these companies closed in from the right without further instruction or command than from the company commander, took their places upon the right of their respective regiments, and went into battle with them. This manner of using skirmishers was found both convenient and effective, and Arnold's battalion was noted for its efficiency, and was sometimes used as an independent, detached command. As such on the evening of the sixteenth it was ordered forward from the left of D. H. Hill's Division, formed on the right of Hood's skirmishers in the East Woods, and engaged the 13th Pennsylvania Reserves of Seymour's brigade. At the close of the engagement, it withdrew to the Roulette orchard and bivouacked. Early on the morning of the 17th the battalion again went forward and deployed along the fence, running from Mumma's barn in the direction of the East Woods, where it engaged the 26th and 94th New York. Upon the retreat of Ricketts' Division and the advance of Hood's Division, it entered the East Woods and engaged the advance of the Twelfth Corps. It claims to have been in action an hour before its brigade became engaged, that it advanced into the woods with the 4th Alabama and continued in action until driven out by Greene's Division.

At about 7 a. m. Colquitt's Brigade moved a short distance along the Sunken Road by the left flank, filed to the right, marched over a grass field, along the east fence of Mumma's cornfield, then, moving north, went over the low ground between Mumma's and Roulette's, passed the burning buildings and the small grave-yard and crossed the Smoketown road at the southwest corner of the woods, where Ripley's Brigade had crossed. Ripley's Brigade though still firing at Gordon's line, was considerably broken and D. H. Hill hastened Colquitt to its support. Still moving by the left flank, the 13th Alabama in advance, it passed the right of the 3rd North Carolina and then obliqued to the left across its front, the 3rd North Carolina, at the same time, obliquing to the left in its rear. When the 13th Alabama, moving in the open ground south of the corn, had gone what was judged to be a sufficient distance to bring the entire brigade in line, in open ground west of the woods and to clear the 4th Alabama, the Georgians and the 5th Texas, in the woods, the four leading regiments were fronted to the right and formed line, but part of the 27th Georgia was in the woods, as was also the 6th Georgia, which was the rear regiment and had entered the woods in crossing the road. Line formed, fire was immediately opened upon Gordon, which was participated in by the left center of Ripley's Brigade. The greater part of the line had the protection of the rock ledges just south of the corn, but parts of the line were much exposed and suffered severely from Gordon's fire which was delivered with great coolness and deadly accuracy. While Colquitt was thus engaged two guns of

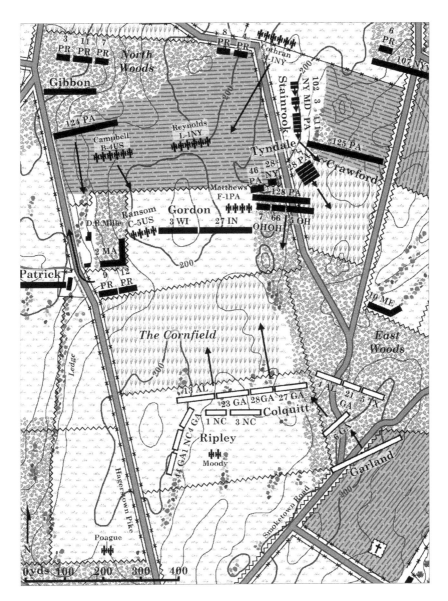

Colquitt deploys in front of Ripley and moves north to engage Gordon.
Garland's Brigade moves north into the East Woods. Greene's division
arrives on the field. Expect for the 13th Alabama and 6th Georgia, the
order of Colquitt's Brigade is unknown due to conflicting primary sources.
Even the Carman-Cope maps differ from his manuscript. Carman's order
from the text is used here.

Captain Moody's Battery, of S. D. Lee's battalion, came up in rear of the 13th Alabama and began firing. When Hood's Division became engaged the contending lines were so close that Lee could not use his artillery, but now he advanced these two guns to the assistance of Ripley and Colquitt.

The 6th Georgia was the last to get on the brigade line. It came under fire, and formed line in the East Woods, engaging the 10th Maine. It did not long tarry with the Maine men, leaving them to Robbins and his mixed command, but went forward, and, as Robbins was in front, obliqued to the left, passed in rear of the 5th Texas, emerged from the woods and came up on the right of the brigade line, then engaged, and all pushed into the cornfield, followed by the 3rd North Carolina and part of the First. When midway through the corn, passing over many dead and wounded men of both sides, it was met by such a terrific fire from Gordon's line that its advance was checked. Officers fell in every regiment and men went down by the score. To advance was impossible and the entire brigade laid down and continued to fire.

Gordon's line, particularly the 3rd Wisconsin and 27th Indiana, was suffering severely. They stood on higher ground than the Confederates, the sky behind them, in good musket range, a good target, not yielding an inch, giving and taking punishment. When first coming into position, Ransom's Battery had been silenced by the persistent and accurate fire of the 3rd North Carolina, and the gunners had gone to the rear, but when Gordon came up, the gunners returned, charged the pieces with canister and added their destructive work to that of the infantry.

Meanwhile Stewart, under Gibbon's order to resume his position of the early morning, had come up and seeing that Ransom occupied the ground, formed on his left, but the 3rd Wisconsin being only a few feet in his immediate front, he could not use his guns. Recognizing the danger of the situation, he sent his limbers and horses to the rear, charged his guns with canister, and the men laid down among them, protected by the slight swell of ground in front, on which stood the 3rd Wisconsin, and resisted the further advance of the enemy. Cothran's New York battery of six guns came up and halted about 150 yards in rear of Ransom; Matthew's Battery was still in position and ready for more work, about 160 yards in rear of the left of the 27th Indiana, and Reynolds' Battery was near.

Colquitt's men were checked about midway in the cornfield, but they had not given up hopes of driving Gordon from the field, and when, after a halt of five to seven minutes, they heard that Garland's Brigade was coming up on the right, they again went forward. The right of the 6th Georgia moved along the edge of the East Woods, and it, and the regiment on its left, reached the north fence of the cornfield, some of the men went over it, but

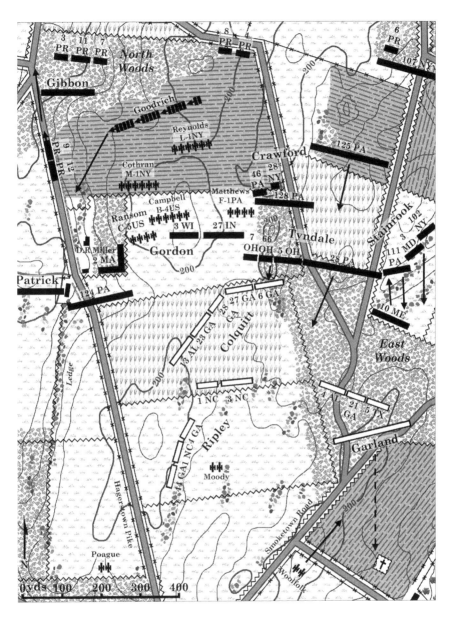

Colquitt engages Gordon and Tyndale at the northern fence of the Cornfield. Garland's Brigade retreats before it enters combat.

were quickly killed or driven back. The three regiments on the left were met by such a rapid and accurate fire that they were checked before reaching the fence and the entire brigade was ordered to lie down and continue the fight until Garland's men could come up on the right. Officers and men saw the dead and severely wounded of Law's Brigade lying along the fence in almost unbroken line. As Colquitt's men advanced Ransom poured canister upon them, the infantry rained bullets among them, and this fire was continued after the brigade had again been checked. From the higher ground where the 3rd Wisconsin stood could be seen a steady stream of Confederate wounded, limping, crawling, or being helped to the rear. The 3rd Wisconsin, also, was suffering severely, and the other regiments were hotly engaged. The 2nd Massachusetts, which had moved into the orchard, about 75 yards in advance of the other regiment, gave a cross-fire across the front of the 3rd Wisconsin and 27th Indiana, which was very effective upon the right of Colquitt's line.

The only Union forces at this time and place engaged, in fact anywhere engaged on the entire field, were the 2nd Massachusetts, 3rd Wisconsin, 27th Indiana, and Ransom's Battery, on Gordon's line, and farther to the left, about 450 yards, the 10th Maine; and at this time the Confederate fire was terribly destructive; it seemed that the Wisconsin and Indiana regiments would be entirely destroyed—they could not be driven—but at this moment, after the 2nd Massachusetts had opened its enfilade fire, a small body of Union men was seen to advance into the East Woods, on the left, and open full upon the flank and front of the 6th Georgia, which fire, with that of Gordon's men, almost annihilated it, and drove the entire brigade from the field. The Union body so opportunely appearing was the advance of Greene's Division and it soon drove the entire Confederate line, with S. D. Lee's artillery, from the field and across the Hagerstown road. Before treating of Greene's action and success we must follow the movements of Garland's Confederate brigade to this part of the field.

Garland's Brigade, commanded by Colonel D. K. McRae, 5th North Carolina, Garland being killed at South Mountain, was composed of the 5th, 12th, 13th, 20th, and 23rd North Carolina, and as near as we can estimate, numbered 756 officers and men. It followed Colquitt from the Sunken Road and formed line near the small grave-yard, where it halted a few minutes, subjected to a severe fire from Union artillery beyond the Antietam, then advanced in line of battle, the 5th North Carolina on the right, across the plowed field and over the fences of the Smoketown road into the East Woods. Here great confusion ensued. Various conflicting orders were passed down the line, the men in the ranks being allowed by the officers to repeat them, so that it became impossible to understand which came from proper authority, and it followed that the movements of the brigade were vacillating and unsteady, obliquing to the right and then

In the East Woods looking north from the area held by the 4th Alabama, 21st Georgia, and 5th Texas. The open area in the background was wooded in 1862 and is currently being replanted. It is highly likely a Confederate used this very boulder as cover during the battle. *Author's collection.*

the left, coming finally upon a ledge of rock and swelling ground, forming a fine natural breastwork. Under cover of this the brigade sought shelter from a scattering fire. It was a little shaky, had not recovered from its severe experience at South Mountain and when the right saw the 28th Pennsylvania coming up in the open field, beyond the woods, and somewhat on the flank, it became very uneasy. Where the right of the 5th North Carolina rested the conformation of the ground was such that a few files were exposed and Captain Garrett ordered these to deploy as flankers to the right and take shelter behind the trees. At this moment, and while directing the movement, Captain Thompson approached Garrett and in a very excited manner and tone cried out: "They are flanking us! See, yonder is a whole brigade." Garrett ordered him to keep silence and return to his place. At the same time a cry ran along the front to cease firing as Ripley's men were in front.

Some men were seen in front, not Ripley's but those of the 4th Alabama and 5th Texas, and the idea that they were firing into them created a very unfavorable impression in the ranks, and, added to the appearance of the enemy on the flank, stampeded the brigade. Some of the brigade retreated to the West Woods, some of it all the way to Sharpsburg, a part of it was rallied in the Sunken Road, and, joined by a part of Colquitt's Brigade, formed on the left of Rodes' Brigade. D. H. Hill says the brigade had been much demoralized by the fight at South Mountain, and that Thompson's indiscreet cry that they were being flanked, "spread like an electric shock, along the ranks, bringing up vivid recollections of the flank fire at South Mountain. In a moment they broke and fled to the rear."

In a letter written December 27, 1870, Colonel McRae says:

> Line was formed facing a woods to our left into which we were directed to advance, being cautioned by General Hill not to fire upon Colquitt, who might be in our front. Very soon after we entered the woods we encountered a fire of what appeared to be a slight skirmish line, when a cry went through the line that these were Colquitt's troops [they were the 10th Maine] and I gave the order for my men to desist firing until I could reconnoiter.... I mounted a rock and looking over the slope for about a hundred yards, I saw a line of what I suppose to be about a regiment with the flag of the United States flying, and I ordered the brigade to fire and charge. But at this moment some scattering troops of the enemy were discovered on our extreme right, and a cry started from that portion of my line, 'They are flanking us,' and in a moment the most unutterable stampede occurred. The whole line vanished and a brigade famed for previous and subsequent conduct of each of its regiments fled in panic from the field, leaving me with one or two officers to get off the field as well as I could.

Looking along the Smoketown Road toward the East Woods. Garland's Brigade fled from the woods in this area, and Lt. Terrell's section of Woolfolk's Battery was captured by Greene's division here. *Author's collection.*

When Garland's Brigade fled the field D. H. Hill was in the Smoketown road, near the corner of the East Woods. Perceiving that Colquitt and Ripley could not make head against Gordon's staunch line, and satisfied of the truth of the report that a Union force was on his flank, and that its movement indicated an attack on the flank and rear of his two brigades, he sent orders for their withdrawal to the Dunker Church, where he proposed to rally and make a stand, and almost immediately thereafter he rode to the front and left to lead them from the field. But he was too late; for Greene's Division was upon them. As he rode to the front two guns of Woolfolk's Battery were coming into the plowed field between Mumma's farm and the East Woods.

As elsewhere stated Greene's Division consisted of three brigades and carried into action 2,504 officers and men. It followed Gordon's Brigade from its brief bivouac on the Hofmann farm, its regiments in column by division; Tyndale's Brigade in advance, followed by Stainrook and Goodrich. It halted two or three times to make coffee and was as often ordered forward without having time to do so. The last time with Mansfield riding up with all speed, very much excited and ordering them to move forward at once, as the enemy was driving Hooker back. Then he rode forward and conducted Crawford's Brigade into action. As Greene followed Gordon a steady stream of Hooker's men was met going to the rear, and when the leading brigade came nearly abreast the north part of the East Woods, Williams rode up, informed Greene that Mansfield had been wounded and directed that Goodrich's Brigade be sent across the Hagerstown road to report to Gibbon, and Greene was ordered to deploy the brigades of Tyndale and Stainrook on the left of the J. Poffenberger lane and advance, swinging his left in the direction of the Mumma buildings, which were still burning. The detachment of Goodrich left Greene 1,727 officers and men in the two brigades; Tyndale having 1,191 and Stainrook 536. Tyndale's largest regiment was the 28th Pennsylvania, which went into action with 29 officers and 766 men. The three Ohio regiments—5th, 7th and 66th—had been so reduced by the casualties and hardships of Pope's campaign that they had an aggregate of 425 officers and men, and it was proposed, just before going into action, to throw the three Ohio flags into one cluster and fight them as a single regiment, but as the third flag would make some confusion and as no regiment was willing to go in without its own colors, the idea was not adopted and each regiment preserved its organization and carried its flag. The 28th Pennsylvania was full and strong for, though an old regiment, Antietam was its first field fight.

In advancing the 7th Ohio was on the right and to its left, in order named, the 66th and 5th Ohio, and 28th Pennsylvania. When reaching the northeast corner of the woods, the 28th Pennsylvania began swinging to

Brigadier General George S. Greene.
Library of Congress.

the right, and also gaining ground to the left, and it was the sight of this large regiment and a scattering fire from the 10th Maine that caused the stampede of Garland's Brigade. While the 28th Pennsylvania was coming into position on the left, the three Ohio regiments deploying to the right, moved toward the right of the line that the 28th Pennsylvania was to take, which brought the 7th and 66th Ohio into the East Woods and immediately in front of the right of Colquitt's Brigade, drawn up along the north fence of the cornfield. Colonel Powell of the 66th Ohio, says the march "was now directed more to the right so as to pass by the strip of woods and into the field beyond" and as they raised a slight hill in the woods, and to within a few rods of the corner of them, still obliquing to the right, Powell, who was riding with Captain Crane, commanding 7th Ohio, near the right of the line, peering into the mist and battle-smoke, which hung low, observed a line of the enemy about 30 yards distant, who, looking steadily and intently to the left, had not yet observed the two regiments. He immediately gave the orders to fire. "No," shouted Crane, "they are our men." Powell, sure that he was not mistaken, urged his horse into the ranks of the 66th Ohio, and succeeded in getting the first volley into the close ranks of the enemy before they could prepare for it.

It was but a moment before that the captain of the 6th Georgia approached Lieutenant Colonel Newton and reported that they were being flanked and instantly both the captain and Newton were killed by the first volley of the 66th Ohio. The 7th Ohio now joined in the fire and Gordon's men poured in heavy volleys, but Colquitt's men stood their ground most manfully. It was not for long, however, for soon they were struck on the right flank and in rear.

When the 28th Pennsylvania had swung around to the right, so that it faced the east part of the woods, and when within 50 yards of them, still closed in mass, it came under a severe fire from the woods, and began its deployment. The 5th Ohio deploying on its right, and orders were sent to the 10th Maine to get out of the way. The Maine men fell back out of the woods and from the fence bordering them and went to the rear. Not a shot was fired by the Pennsylvania regiment until the fourth division was fully uncovered and the alignment perfected; then a volley was fired "which sounded like one gun," and the regiment, with the 5th Ohio on its right and the 111th Pennsylvania, of Stainrook's Brigade, on its left, dashed into the woods and drove out Robbins' men, who, since Hood's first advance, had so stubbornly held their position, contending both with the 10th Maine on their right and on their front and left with such Union troops as appeared in the north part of the woods and in the lower part of the field west of them. The 4th Alabama had come under a left oblique fire from the Ohio regiments, who were contending with Colquitt's right; it had already lost one-half its men in killed and wounded, and it, with the Georgians on the

Northeast corner of the Cornfield fence and the position of the 6th Georgia from the perspective of the three small Ohio regiments in Tyndale's brigade. *Author's collection.*

right, fell back obliquely to the right and rear through the woods, soon followed by the 5th Texas. Captain Turner, commanding the 5th Texas, had four times sent to Hood for support, and had as often been informed that it could not be given and that he must hold on and about the time Hood's last message came the right of Garland's Brigade came up and took position on his right, when, the 28th Pennsylvania advancing, Garland's men fired their wild volley, broke and ran. The Texans were now nearly out of ammunition, the 4th Alabama and the Georgians were giving way on the left, the Union line was closing in on the right, and, as the volley of the 28th Pennsylvania was delivered, Turner gave the order to fall back, but not soon enough to prevent the capture of some of his men. In the charge into the woods the 5th Ohio and the right wing of the 28th Pennsylvania pushed straight to the east fence of the cornfield, and after firing four or five volleys into corn, which swept down Colquitt's line, charged into it as the 7th and 66th Ohio cleared the north fence of the cornfield. Powell says:

> The sight at the fence, where the enemy was standing, when we gave our first fire, was awful beyond description; dead men were literally piled upon and across each other. We had been enabled to pour a volley into an entire line, at a few rods distance and striking them in the flank at about the same time. No line of men in the world, of equal strength, could have done better than they tried to do, or have recovered from the situation. The circumstances were all against them, and thus they had to go down.

The fighting in the northeast corner of the corn was now fast and furious and hand to hand, bayonets were used by those who had them, and those who had not used clubbed guns; the 6th Georgia holding the right of the line was almost wiped out of existence, the rest of the brigade was suffering severely, the left wing of the 28th Pennsylvania was swinging up in its rear and it broke and went back leaving many prisoners in the hands of its enemy, and an appalling number of dead and wounded on field, with the victors in close pursuit.

When Garland's men stampeded and D. H. Hill ordered Colquitt's and Ripley's men to withdraw and rode to the left to conduct the movement, he succeeded in getting the left of Ripley's started for the Dunker Church, in good order, but the 3rd North Carolina and part of the First were involved in Colquitt's disaster. They had followed Colquitt into the corn, and in the second line, had come under Gordon's fire. They were obliquing to the left, with the intention of forming on the 13th Alabama, the left of Colquitt's line, when Tyndale's Brigade made its attack and forced Colquitt from the field, the retreating men passing both flanks of the two North Carolina regiments. Effort was made to stay the precipitate retreat, and make

Northeast corner of the Cornfield fence where the 6th Georgia was flanked and shattered. View from inside the woods and the Union perspective looking west. *Author's collection.*

headway against the enemy, but it was unavailing and the North Carolinians retreated to woods around the Dunker Church.

While the 5th Ohio and right wing of the 28th Pennsylvania went through the woods and into the corn, sweeping everything before them, the left wing of the 28th Pennsylvania and the 111th, on its left, did not make such rapid progress, for the 4th Alabama and the 5th Texas were falling back but a short distance, made a stand and poured in such an annoying fire on the flank of the line, that it was momentarily checked. A short and sharp contest ensued, a half wheel made to the left, Robbins and his men were driven farther toward the southern part of the woods, when they came under the fire of the 3rd Maryland and 102nd New York, and the Pennsylvanians going forward came out of the East Woods and into the open ground south of the corn, as the three Ohio regiments and the right wing of the 28th Pennsylvania broke Colquitt's line and started in pursuit. The brigade was now united, the 111th Pennsylvania still on its left, and advanced; Colquitt's men made a stand at several points to resist them, Moody's two guns, which were near the south edge of the corn, when the break came, fell back sullenly, going into position two or three times and opening full in the face and on the flank of their pursuers; Colquitt made several efforts to rally his men along the fences of the Smoketown road, but was not successful, and the three Ohio regiments crossing the Smoketown Road about midway from the Mumma lane to the Dunker Church, under a severe artillery fire, took shelter in the low ground between the Mumma house and the Dunker Church. The 28th and 111th Pennsylvania crossed the Smoketown road between the woods and the Mumma lane, captured the two guns of Woolfolk's Battery, that had fired but two shots and then been abandoned, and, crossing Mumma's lane, joined the Ohio regiments. Here they awaited ammunition, and the 3rd Maryland and 102nd New York came up and formed on their left.

While the 28th Pennsylvania was deploying north of the Smoketown road, preparatory to its advance into the East Woods, Stainrook's Brigade was marching on its left to deploy south of the road. After crossing the road the 111th Pennsylvania deployed in good shape, advanced firing, its right on the road, came up to and went forward with the 28th Pennsylvania, but the 3rd Maryland and 102nd New York, on the left, after crossing the road and being ordered to deploy under fire became intermingled and confused. The right of the 102nd New York was run into by the 3rd Maryland, its left came under a severe skirmish fire from the woods and gave back, for a time disorder reigned supreme, but some of the officers sprang to the front, the men were rallied and, on a run, with the 3rd Maryland on its right, the regiment went over the fence and dashed into the East Woods, taking Texans, Georgians, and Alabamians prisoners. The 5th Texas escaped by going down the Smoketown road before the Ohio men

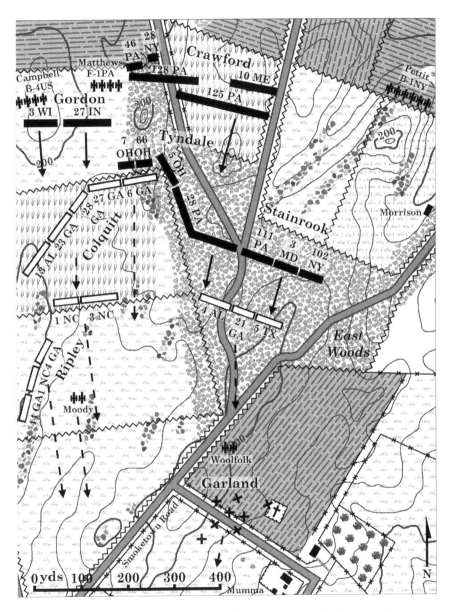

Tyndale's brigade flanks Colquitt, devastating the 6th Georgia. Both brigades of Greene's division advance, driving the Confederates from the Cornfield and the East Woods.

reached it; Robbins, with the remnant of the 4th Alabama, went south, beyond the Mumma buildings, and thence to the Dunker Church, where Stonewall Jackson, D. H. Hill, Hood and others were endeavoring to rally the broken lines to dispute the possession of the woods about the church. After passing through the East Woods the 102nd New York and 3rd Maryland crossed the plowed field, until nearing Mumma's the Maryland regiment moved to the right and joined the 111th Pennsylvania, while the 102nd New York, passing to the left of the burning barn, halted near the burning house, from which a greater part of the men, filled with the ardor of pursuit, followed the retreating enemy to the north fence of Mumma's cornfield and began to tear down the fence, some went into the corn, but the great body of them halted at the fence and opened fire on Patterson's Georgia battery, to the right and front, about 30 yards beyond the corn, playing energetically on the right of Greene's Division line. The battery was soon silenced and driven beyond the Hagerstown road, and the regiment, crossing Mumma's lane, took position on the left of its brigade.

General Greene was not popular with his men, but the signal ability with which he had handled his command won their admiration and confidence. The brilliant service performed by his division was surpassed by it later in the morning and shall be noted; meanwhile we return to Gordon's men and other commands, Union and Confederate.

When Greene's men charged into the corn on the left Gordon was compelled to suspend fire; when the Confederate line broke, the three regiments fixed bayonets and pursued, went down through the corn, the 2nd Massachusetts picked up the colors of the 11th Mississippi, and all, wheeling to the right, charged toward the Hagerstown road, with the intention of crossing it, but upon reaching the foot of the rise of ground near the road were halted and ordered to lie down. The 124th Pennsylvania, supported by the Purnell Legion, entered the corn on the right of Gordon, the 125th and parts of the 46th and 128th Pennsylvania charged through the East Woods close on the heels of Greene's men, the 13th New Jersey and 107th New York, that were in reserve, were ordered to the front; batteries were rushed forward and opened upon the West Woods, and Hooker made hurried preparation to follow up the advantage gained by the Twelfth Corps, but, before his preparations were completed, was wounded and borne from the field.

The advantage won by the Twelfth Corps was not without loss. Crawford's regiments engaged had suffered to some extent, as had the 2nd Massachusetts; the 27th Indiana had 209 killed and wounded of the 443 carried into action, and of the 340 taken into action by the 3rd Wisconsin, 27 were killed and 173 wounded, in the aggregate nearly 59 per cent of the number engaged. Greene's loss was not heavy.

Colquitt's Brigade line in the Cornfield. It stretched at an angle from just left of the frame toward the fence at the northern edge of the field, and then the 6th Georgia continued along the fence into the East Woods. *Author's collection.*

On the side of the Confederates, Garland's Brigade got away with slight loss, but Ripley and Colquitt suffered greatly. Out of the 1,349 officers and men taken into action by Ripley 110 were killed, 506 wounded, and 124 missing, an aggregate of 740, being over 50 per cent. Of those engaged, the heaviest loss fell on the 3rd North Carolina, which is officially reported as having 46 killed and 207 wounded, but the muster rolls of the regiment say: "the regiment suffered severely, losing over 300 officers and men."

In his official report Colonel Colquitt says:

At 7 o'clock [8][7] in the morning my brigade entered the fight. It was moved to the front and formed on the right of General Ripley's Brigade, which was then engaged. After a few rounds had been discharged, I ordered an advance, and at the same time sent word to the regiment on my left to advance simultaneously. The order was responded to with spirit by my men, and, with a shout, they moved through the cornfield in front 200 [245][8] yards wide, and formed on the line of a fence. The enemy was near and in full view. In a moment or two his lines began to break before our fire, and the line soon disappeared under the crest of the hill upon which it had been established. It was soon replaced by another, and the fire opened with renewed vigor.

In the meantime General Garland's Brigade, which had been ordered to my right, had given way, and the enemy was advancing, unchecked. The regiments on my left also having failed to advance, we were exposed to a fire from all sides and nearly surrounded. I sent in haste to the rear for reinforcements, and communicated to General Hill the exposed condition of my men. With steady support on our right we could yet maintain our position. The support was not at hand and could not reach us in time. The enemy closed in upon the right so near that our ranks were scarcely distinguishable. At the same time his line in front advanced. My men stood firm until every field officer but one had fallen, and then made the best of their way out. In this sharp and unequal contest I lost many of my best officers and one-half of the men in the ranks. If the brigades upon the right and left had advanced, we should have driven the enemy from the field. He had at one time broken in our front, but we had not strength to push the advantage.

[7] Carman wrote in "8" to modify the time in the report.
[8] Carman wrote in "245" to modify the distance in the report.

Ruins of the Mumma Farm immediately after the battle. *Library of Congress.*

General D. H. Hill says:

> Colquitt had gone in with 10 field officers; 4 were killed, 5 badly wounded, and the tenth had been stunned by a shell. The men were beginning to fall back and efforts were made to rally them in the bed of an old road, nearly at right angles to the Hagerstown road, and which had been their position previous to the advance. These efforts, however, were only partially successful. Most of the brigade took no further part in the action.

It is not surprising that the brigade took no further part in the action, for the loss in some of the regiments was appalling, and the brigade was demoralized by it. It went into action with 1,320 officers and men, and from the official report we gather that it lost 111 killed, 444 wounded, 167 missing, an aggregate of 722, about 55 per cent of those engaged. This includes Arnold's skirmish battalion, engaged in the East Woods. The heaviest loss fell on the 6th Georgia, which held the right of the brigade line and was almost enveloped by the Union advance. Colonel Folsom, in *Heroes and Martyrs of Georgia* writes:

> Our loss [6th Georgia] on this field was almost incredible. We went into battle with not more than 250 men and of the number 81 were left dead, 115 wounded, and about 30 taken prisoner"; or over 81 per cent. The two field officers who led it into action were killed and nearly all of the company officers were killed or wounded. Company C had 27 men in action, and lost 10 killed, 10 wounded, and 5 prisoners; Company E had 33 men in action, of whom 13 were killed, 17 wounded and 3 captured, not an officer or man escaped. Company K had 36 engaged, 15 killed, 15 wounded, and 3 missing. The large proportion of killed is remarkable.

When our attention was called to the statement by Colonel Folsom we communicated with surviving officers and men of the regiment. From three companies we obtained full and accurate information, from the other companies our information was conflicting, but from what we did obtain, leads to the conclusion that the loss of the regiment was nearly or quite 90 per cent, mostly in killed and wounded, and that Colonel Folsom does not overstate it.

The 23rd Georgia had its colonel killed and Lieutenant-Colonel and Major wounded, and half the entire regiment killed and wounded. The Colonel of the 27th Georgia was killed, the Lieutenant-Colonel wounded; every commissioned officer, but one, killed or wounded, and it lost over one-third its enlisted men. The 28th Georgia lost nearly half its 220 officers

Colonel (later Brigadier General) Alfred H. Colquitt.
Library of Congress.

and men, and the 13th Alabama lost a large percentage of its 300 men. The loss of the brigade was much greater than that stated in the official reports.

When battle began in the morning Colonel Stephen D. Lee had four batteries of his battalion on the plateau opposite the Dunker Church, all of which opened fire at daylight, over the heads of the Confederates, upon the Union artillery and infantry with good effect. Two guns of Jordan's Battery, as we have seen, were very early sent to an advanced position on the line of Trimble's Brigade. Here, mixed in with the infantry, they were exposed to an infantry fire from the East Woods, not over 200 yards distant, and to the fire of the heavy guns beyond the Antietam, and of Thompson's and Matthews' guns near D. R. Miller's. They were disabled in a half hour and obliged to retire. Meanwhile the other guns kept up continuous fire upon the batteries of Thompson and Matthews and upon Hooker's infantry, as it advanced to the attack and in position south of the corn, until Hood's Division advanced, when the contending lines were so close that the firing ceased. His batteries were exposed to an enfilade fire of more than 20 rifled guns beyond the Antietam, from Thompson and Matthews in front, and from the fire of the Union infantry, both from the front and the East Woods on the right. His men and horses suffered very heavily and Rhett's Battery was ordered to the rear for ammunition, and Parker's and Woolfolk's slightly to the rear to refit, many men and horses being killed. So many horses had been killed or disabled that the pieces could be moved only by leaving the caissons. About this time Moody's Battery, which had been engaged near the center of D. H. Hill's line, arrived and reported. Lee placed it in position on the ground previously occupied by Parker, and two guns of Blackshear's Battery, Cutts' Battalion, under Lieutenant Thomas Maddox, came up and went on the left of Woolfolk's Battery. Hood's Division now began to fall back, but the lines were so close that it was impossible for Lee to use his guns, and he advanced one of Moody's sections beyond the Smoketown road and very nearly to Miller's cornfield, where he could use it. The section remained in this position and did good service for about ten minutes, under Captain Moody and Lieutenant John B. Gorey, exposed to a galling infantry fire, and until Colquitt's Brigade gave way, when it was ordered to the rear, Moody stopping several times to fire as he fell back. Gorey was shot in the head by a musket ball and instantly killed as he was sighting his gun for a last shot.

When D. H. Hill advanced his brigades Lieutenant Maddox, commanding Blackshear's section, had been wounded, and Sergeant-Major Robert Falligant took charge of the section. He was ordered by Lee to advance to the right where he fired until compelled to stop by Hill's advance, lest he should fire into his rear.

Very soon after Moody's two guns were ordered beyond the Smoketown road to the assistance of Ripley and Colquitt, two guns of Woolfolk's

Confederate artillery casualties from S. D. Lee's battalion on the ridge across the Hagerstown Turnpike from the Dunker Church. *Library of Congress.*

Battery, under command of Lieutenant W. D. Terrell, were ordered to the right. Terrell left his caissons behind the Mumma stacks and advanced his guns into the plowed field beyond the grave-yard. He fired but two rounds of canister at Greene's men as they came out of the East Woods and abandoned the guns to the 28th Pennsylvania.

When Colquitt and Ripley began to give way Lee's guns were ordered by D. H. Hill to the ridge west of the Hagerstown road and about 600 yards southwest of the church, where they fired for a short time at Greene's men, who had advanced to the ground just vacated by them. Here they remained until McLaws came up when they moved back about a mile to the right. We shall see them again late in the day, but may here say that they had suffered so severely in this morning engagement that but 12 guns could be brought into the action when they again went to the front on Cemetery Hill and ridge.

Early in the engagement a section of Blackshear's Battery was in position on the right of the Hagerstown road, near the left of Lawton's Brigade, from which position it was driven by Gibbon's advance and formed on the right of Woolfolk's Battery, nearly opposite the church, and Patterson's guns were advanced, facing the Union line, nearly opposite the church. A few minutes before Hill's line broke he ordered Patterson to watch the line and if it broke to bring out the guns. It fell back as Hill's line began to give way and took position a few yards in rear of Mumma's cornfield, from which position it was soon driven by the 102nd New York and fell back across the Hagerstown road on the left of Rodes' Brigade, which had just formed in the Sunken Road.

All the Confederates north of the Sunken Road had now been driven across the Hagerstown road and we return to the movements that had occurred west of the road, since the repulse of Starke's men and the fight of Gibbon, Patrick and Hood around Stewart's guns, near the straw stacks, and to some events still earlier in the day.

In the preceding chapter, we have briefly noted the action, early in the morning, of the Confederate batteries on the left, with the batteries of Doubleday's Division. At this time Balthis', Wooding's and Carpenter's batteries were in or near the edge of the cornfield that crowned the Nicodemus hill; Balthis' in the northeast corner of a field, joining the cornfield on the south, Wooding's and Carpenter's in the cornfield. Pelham's Battery was about (?)[9] yards to the right of Balthis. The Union fire upon these four batteries was very accurate and effective and they were

[9] Left blank by Carman. Clemens puts the distance at 50 yards. Thomas G. Clemens, *The Maryland Campaign of September 1862: Vol. II: Antietam* (El Dorado Hills: Savas Beatie, 2012), p. 147.

Confederate dead south of the Smoketown Road. This view is looking southwest. The Dunker Church would be over the slight rise to the right off the camera frame. *Library of Congress.*

soon temporarily silenced. Wooding's was ordered to the rear about sunrise. Carpenter's was soon withdrawn to the cover of the ridge, as was Balthis', which was moved farther to the left. They were not permanently withdrawn from action, but as the Union fire slackened, they would be run forward and open fire upon the advancing infantry of Hooker and Mansfield, again to be driven back. They had some assistance from Brockenbrough's and D'Aquin's batteries, which, by Jackson's orders, had gone to the left, and by some guns of Cutts' Battalion. Stuart reports that when the enemy had advanced too far into the woods near the Dunker Church for the fire to be continued without danger of harming his own friends he withdrew the batteries farther to the rear, but Early says they were withdrawn because a body of the enemy's troops were making their way gradually between the batteries and the left of the main infantry line. The position to which they were withdrawn was on the Hauser ridge, near the Hauser house, nearly due west of the Dunker Church.

Pelham's Battery, supported by the 13th Virginia Infantry and a small cavalry force, was left near the northwest corner of the West Woods. D'Aquin's Battery fell back to Cox's for ammunition. J. R. Johnson's Battery, which encamped on the night of the 16th in open ground, west of the south part of the West Woods, entered the woods about 4 a.m. of the 17th and remained there until Lawton had been repulsed, when it was ordered to the rear to find water for the horses, and Raine's Battery fell back to the ridge near Hauser's.

When Poague retired from the fight, early in the morning, to the A. Poffenberger barn and joined the other guns of his battery and those of Raine, he was exposed to a cross-fire of heavy artillery on the right by which one man was mortally wounded; then about 7 a.m., he moved his entire battery back about 300 yards and to the left near the crest of the Hauser ridge, so as to command the West Woods in case the infantry should be compelled to abandon them. Having reported to Jackson he was directed to advance toward the Hagerstown road and see if a battery would be of any assistance in that direction, or on the road, but finding all of the eligible positions already occupied, he proceeded to a position in rear of that occupied by him in the early morning, and quite close to the woods and the Hagerstown road. There was no infantry in the field, but a gap in the line of some 200 yards between Early's right, who had just taken position, and the left of D. H. Hill's forces, then engaged east of the road. Two guns were all he had with him, these opened first to the front on the Union line, but Ripley and Colquitt soon giving way and the Union line advancing on the flank he withdrew the guns through the woods and resumed his position on the ridge near Hauser's. This was after 8 o'clock and Jackson was near making efforts to stop the stream of stragglers pouring east of the West Woods.

View from Stuart's cavalry toward Nicodemus Hill, which is obscured by the trees at the opposite end of the field, and the location of the 10th Pennsylvania Reserves, which would have been at the right of the frame across the field. *Author's collection.*

During the night of the 16th the 7th Virginia Cavalry of Munford's Brigade took position near Ground Squirrel Church, on the Hagerstown road, about 900 yards north of Doubleday's brigades. Early in the morning it discovered that it was in false position, a squadron of the 3rd Pennsylvania Cavalry in its front and Doubleday's infantry in its rear, upon which it retreated to the southwest to New Industry on the Potomac, where it remained until late in the forenoon, when it moved south and joined its brigade near the Blackford house, about a mile south of Sharpsburg.

When Hooker's artillery opened fire on the Confederate batteries on Nicodemus hill those were supported by Fitz-Hugh Lee's cavalry, which had bivouacked in the valley in their rear, near Cox's house, some of it in an orchard and some in open ground adjoining. Fitz Lee remained in support of the guns until relieved by Early's infantry brigade when he moved farther to the left, out of range of the artillery fire, and massed his regiments near the river, picketing well to the left and guarding that flank, but was not actually engaged during the morning. The 9th Virginia Cavalry was detached early in the day and reported to Jackson, near the Reel house, southwest of the church, by whom it was ordered to stop the infantry stragglers who, singly and in groups, were going to the rear. Men without ammunition and many with it were leisurely retiring toward Sharpsburg and some of the Confederate batteries, having shot their last round, were leaving the field at a gallop. All these Jackson ordered stopped and supplied with ammunition from the ordnance train near Reel's and then marched back to the line of battle or conducted to their proper commander. Jackson, motioning to a captain of the 9th, to give him his ear, directed him in a whisper, not to halt any of Hood's men, as they had liberty to retire. The regiment was on that duty the greater part of the day.

So soon as notified that Starke was killed, Grigsby, who succeeded to the command of Jackson's Division, endeavored to reform the commands and restore order, in the border of the woods near the A. Poffenberger buildings, and while so engaged Early came up.

At the time Hays' Brigade was ordered by Lawton to move to the assistance of the line east of the Hagerstown road, Early was ordered by Jackson, in person, to march his brigade to the left and support Stuart's artillery, then engaged with Hooker's batteries on the J. Poffenberger hill. Early moved through a piece of woods northwest of the A. Poffenberger, a little back from the left of the line, and then through some fields, and as he was passing through these fields he discovered Union skirmishers moving around the left, upon which he sent some from his own brigade to hold them in check until he had passed. He found Stuart nearly three-fourths of a mile to the left with several guns in position on Nicodemus hill, supported by a squadron of the 5th Virginia Cavalry, and engaged with Hooker's guns. At Stuart's suggestion he formed his brigade in line in rear of the crest of

The destroyed Reel barn after the battle. *Library of Congress.*

the hill and remained there about an hour, under artillery fire by which some of his men were killed and wounded, when Stuart, his batteries suffering severely, having discovered that Patrick and Gibbon were gradually making their way between him and the left of the main line, determined to shift his position to an eminence nearer Jackson's line and a little bit to the rear, on the Hauser ridge, and, under Stuart's instructions, Early moved back, taking a route in rear of the one by which he had moved out, and then into the skirt of woods through which he had passed, an hour or more before, the woods about 425 yards northwest of A. Poffenberger, but just as he was getting into line Stuart informed him that Lawton had been wounded and that Jackson had sent for him to carry his brigade back and take command of the division. Leaving the 13th Virginia, numbering less than 100 men, with Stuart, at his request, to skirmish with the 10th Pennsylvania Reserves, which had relieved the 23rd New York, and to support one of his batteries, Early moved to the rear of the woods, and passed the south edge of a cornfield lying east of them; as he came near where he had bivouacked the night before, he found Grigsby and Stafford rallying some 200 to 300 men of Jackson's Division, where Starke's Brigade had lain the night before. As he came up Grigsby advanced and Early, forming his brigade in line, followed him, Patrick falling back from the ledge parallel to the road to one beyond Miller's barn and perpendicular to the road. Early halted at a ridge or rock ledge, running east and west in the woods, which protected the right of the brigade and Grigsby, who had advanced on open ground was now moved to Early's left, forming a diagonal line, the left occupying a hollow in the south edge of the northern body of the West Woods, and the 31st Virginia of Early's Brigade was put on Grigsby's right.

Early's line when thus formed was 130 yards from the north edge of the central body of the West Woods and perpendicular to the Hagerstown road, his right resting near the open plateau between the woods and the road, concealed and protected by the rise of the ground. The 49th Virginia, on the right, faced the Hagerstown road, being formed at right angles to the main brigade line. Patrick's Brigade was seen in the field in his north front, threatening his flank and rear and skirmishers were sent to the edge of the woods in which he lay and to the left.

These precautions taken, and as Patrick showed no disposition to advance, in fact he was making coffee, Early directed Colonel William Smith, 49th Virginia, to take command of the brigade, resist Patrick should he advance, and then rode across the Hagerstown road to take command of the rest of the division and ascertain its condition. Early's Brigade was composed of seven Virginia regiments, the 13th, 25th, 31st, 44th, 49th, 52nd and 58th, and numbered 1,225 officers and men. The 13th, a small body of less than 100 men, had been detached earlier in the day and as now

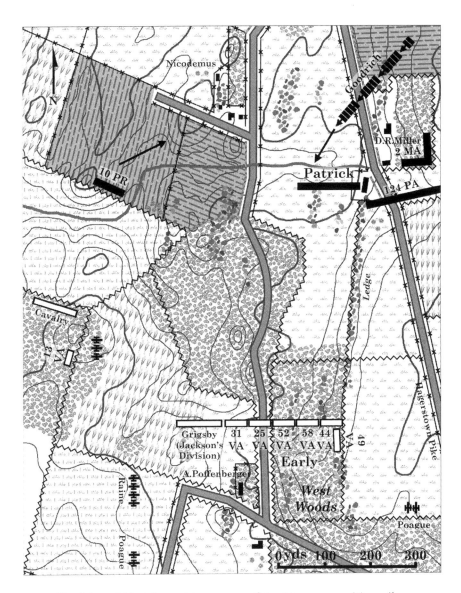

Patrick and Early's positions west of the Hagerstown Turnpike.

formed the rest of the brigade was in line from right to left in this order: 49th, 44th, 58th, 25th, and 31st, the last named being on the right of Jackson's Division. Early made his report of the Maryland campaign January 12, 1863, in which he says:

> I hope I may be excused for referring to the record shown by my own brigade, which has never been broken or compelled to fall back or left one of its dead to be buried by the enemy, but has invariably driven the enemy when opposed to him, and slept upon the ground on which its has fought, in every action, with the solitary exception of the affair at Bristoe Station, where it retired under orders.

When Early rode in search of his division he found that it had fallen back some distance to the rear to organize; heard that it was greatly shattered and would not probably be in condition again to be engaged, but sent a staff officers[sic] to find the brigades and order them up. While looking for Trimble's, Lawton's and Hays' brigades Early saw that Ripley and Colquitt were giving way, and he rode to Jackson, informed him of the condition of his division, and that the enemy was advancing on the west side of the Hagerstown road, on the flank on which he had formed his brigade. Jackson assured him that he would send reinforcements and directed him to keep the enemy in check until they arrived, upon which he returned to his brigade and resumed command. Soon after this Goodrich's Brigade of the Twelfth Corps, supported by Patrick advanced, there was a short contest, and Early sent his chief of staff to inform Jackson that danger was imminent. The staff officer returned with Jackson's assurance that reinforcements should be given immediately, and just as he returned Monroe's Battery (1st Rhode Island) opened fire from a position on his right and rear. He took it for granted that it was a Confederate battery, but was soon undeceived when he saw that it was on the plateau opposite the church, firing in the direction of Sharpsburg, and supported by infantry. This convinced him that the Confederates had been driven back on the right, and the Union forces were in entire possession of the field east of the Hagerstown road.

About this time the 124th Pennsylvania, that had advanced from the North Woods, followed Gordon's men and entered the Miller cornfield on their right, one company in and on the right of the Hagerstown road, the entire regiment being under the fire of a Confederate battery beyond the West Woods. After going about 20 yards into the corn it was halted and ordered to lie down. Here Colonel Hawley was wounded by a fire from beyond the road and the regiment fell back to the north fence of the cornfield. In a few minutes it again advanced, supported by the Purnell Legion, and three companies under Major Haldeman, obliquing to the right,

Burying Confederate dead after the battle. Photo taken near the southwest corner of the Cornfield looking northwest. The top of the Miller barn on the west side of the Hagerstown pike is visible the right. *Library of Congress.*

advanced to the right of the road, seven companies continuing the march through the corn. The left of these companies moved close to the road and when about 230 yards beyond the straw stacks the line was fired upon by Grigsby's men in the woods and by artillery beyond them, causing the right to swing back, thus forming an oblique line to the road, and lying down in this position they returned Early's fire for a few minutes, when they fell back into the road and down the road to the stacks. While lying in the road, sheltered by its bank, Sedgwick's Division crossed and went into the West Woods. The seven companies went through the corn to the grassfield beyond, were met by a shower of bullets from the west of the road, and lying down under the cover of the ridge nearly parallel with the road. The Purnell Legion came up and formed on the right and rear of the seven companies.

When Patrick, after the repulse of Jackson's and Hood's divisions, fell back to the ledge near Miller's barn to make coffee, replenish ammunition and await reinforcements, he was soon thereafter fired upon by Pelham's Battery, and to shield his men as much as possible, he was about to enter the woods, some 15 rods yard distant, when Goodrich's Brigade of the Twelfth Corps came up. It will be remembered that this brigade was detached from the rear of Greene's Division as it approached the East Woods. It moved quickly across the field in rear of Gordon's Brigade, crossed the Hagerstown road north of D. R. Miller's house, where the Purnell Legion was detached to support the 124th Pennsylvania, passed Miller's barn and approached the West Woods. The brigade numbered 777 officers and men; by the detachment of the Purnell Legion, it was reduced to three regiments, aggregating 572 officers and men.

Goodrich had been detached at Gibbon's earnest request to save his battery and had been ordered to report to Gibbon or any general officer on that part of the field. The battery had gone and so had Gibbon, and, as Goodrich was approaching the woods, Patrick and his officers cautioned him, advised him of the nature of the ground, the position of the enemy, and gave him some advice how to enfilade and drive Early from his strong position among the rocks in the woods. Patrick says: "Knowing the ground well I directed Colonel Goodrich to advance cautiously, forming his skirmishers, until I could get reinforcements to go in on his left and front in sufficient force to drive through the corner, where the enemy appeared to hold in masses. Riding up the hill to find Doubleday, and through the cornfield to the plowed ground beyond, I found that the enemy had been driven down the road, but not by that point of wood," the corner of the middle wood held by Early.

Goodrich did not wait for Patrick's return. He sent the 3rd Delaware to the front and left as skirmishers and advanced, bearing more to the right than was proper, and entered the woods with the 60th and 78th New York,

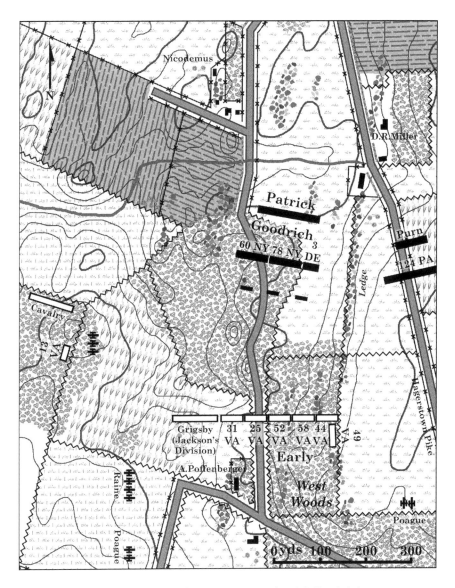

Goodrich advances toward the West Woods with Patrick in support.

followed by the 21st, 23rd and 35th New York, of Patrick's Brigade, as support. In the advance Goodrich was killed, his regiments suffered severely from the fire of Early and Grigsby and were checked. When Patrick returned, without reinforcements, Goodrich was dead and his small brigade with difficulty holding position. Patrick ordered Goodrich's men and his own to hold on, until further orders, confronting Early and Grigsby, who showed no disposition to advance, but, concealed from view, held their ground, and kept up a desultory fire upon Goodrich's skirmishers and the few men of the 124th Pennsylvania in the Hagerstown road.

Just before the Confederates were driven from the field east of the Hagerstown road, Hofmann, where his brigade had been kept in support of the artillery on the Poffenberger hill, was ordered to send two rifled guns across the Hagerstown road. He sent two guns of Cooper's Battery, under Lieutenant Fullerton, supported by the 95th New York, Major Edward Pye. The guns and infantry support took position in a cornfield about 200 yards west of the road and in front of the right of Hofmann's Brigade. As soon as these guns were in position they opened fire upon the enemy, who had withdrawn beyond the range of the howitzers, and soon drew the Confederate fire, which was partially the object of putting the guns in that position. During this time Hofmann's Brigade remained in the position taken the night before, lying close to the fence and well sheltered.

When Colquitt and Ripley were repulsed the Union batteries which had been engaged on the line were in no condition to follow and were ordered to the rear to refit, and Monroe's Rhode Island battery and Edgell's New Hampshire battery were ordered to advance from the Poffenberger hill. They came down through the North Woods and Hooker instructed Monroe to go beyond the cornfield, and as near the woods at the Dunker Church as possible, and that he would find Greene's infantry there to support him. Monroe, closely followed by Edgell, went down a path through the East Woods and into battery on the open ground about 160 yards from the East Woods, his right near the corn, his left extending toward Mumma's gate, on the Smoketown road, the guns facing the Dunker Church and the plateau opposite, and, when taking position, a regiment was seen on the right, with its left refused, the 124th Pennsylvania, and still farther to the right, in the corn, was seen Gordon's Brigade. This seemed to the officers a poor position for the battery, and it had scarcely taken position when the 125th Pennsylvania came out of the East Woods on its left and rear, and an officer of Hooker's staff rode up and ordered Monroe to go forward on the plateau opposite the church. The caissons were left and the guns went to the Smoketown road and halted, until the 125th Pennsylvania removed the fences, when Monroe went forward. As he rose the north slope of the plateau he saw a little to the left and front Greene's infantry lying on the ground, as though expecting an attack. From

Lt. Edgell's 1st New Hampshire Battery position looking toward the hill where Stephen D. Lee had his artillery battalion throughout the morning to the left, and the Dunker Church in the center (partially obscured by trees and the Maryland state monument). *Author's collection.*

their position Monroe judged that there must be a strong force of the enemy in the immediate front, and was much in doubt, whether it was judicious to put his battery in so advanced a position. He rode to the men and asked who they were. Greene now rode up and when asked to support the battery, which had now crossed the road, replied in a low tone that he had no ammunition but most of his men had bayonets. Monroe thought it a strange place for men without ammunition, and that if they could hold on with empty cartridge boxes, he ought to be able to do it with packed limber chests and gave the order "In battery," which was instantly done, the right being on the ground sloping towards the church and about 70 yards from the Hagerstown road, the left section being upon higher ground. The line was perpendicular to the road, the guns pointing south, towards Sharpsburg. Greene's men lay down 30 to 50 yards behind the battery, and Edgell's Battery came up on the left and about 100 yards in the rear. As the battery went into position a Confederate battery was dropping its guns into battery not over 250 yards distant.

When Greene's Division charged through the East Woods and then across the Smoketown road, in pursuit of Colquitt's men, the 125th Pennsylvania was lying in the open ground east of the East Woods and while here, Higgins says: "General Mansfield fell, some of my men carrying him off the field on their muskets until a blanket was procured." Sometime after Greene's charge the regiment was ordered forward; went through the East Woods, its right going through the southeast corner of the cornfield and came into the open ground, where it halted for alignment, its left on and beyond the Smoketown road. Colonel Higgins reports:

> Here I took some prisoners, whom I sent to the rear. Again I was ordered to advance and halt in line with a battery. Before reaching the battery, though, I took a number of prisoners, some of whom came running back with white handkerchiefs tied on their guns and gave themselves up. At the battery I gave the command for my men to lie down whilst awaiting further orders. About this time the fire of the enemy slackened somewhat, only some shots from their sharpshooters being fired, and these at mounted officers and the artillery horses.

It was while at this halt that the men removed the fences for the passage of Monroe's Battery across the Smoketown road and it appears they performed the same service for Edgell's New Hampshire battery. Hooker now rode up and asked Higgins if any troops were in the West Woods in front to which Higgins replied, "none but rebels," and that the 125th Pennsylvania was in front of the Union line. While talking to Higgins, Hooker's horse was shot, and Higgins called his attention to it, he turned and rode away, in the direction of the East Woods. The 107th New York,

Colonel Stephen D. Lee's view from his artillery battalion position. Greene's division of the Twelfth Corps exited the East Woods in the left background and advanced across this open ground toward his position. *Author's collection.*

which had deployed along the border of the S. Poffenberger woods, followed soon after the 125th Pennsylvania, charging in line of battle through the East Woods, and halted with its right wing in the Smoketown road, west of the woods, its left wing in the East Woods. It faced southeast.

It was about this time that Hooker, riding back from the 125th Pennsylvania to get more artillery, was painfully wounded in the foot and obliged to give up his command. He says:

> At 9 o'clock that morning I had advanced steadily, but securely, to the point that I desired. I had at that time a battery of howitzers (Monroe's) on this high ground. I had sent for two additional batteries to double-quick up to that position. A number of my infantry regiments were well posted to protect them on their arrival. While advancing, on the morning of the 17th, and about half-past 7 o'clock, Mansfield's Corps, at my request, had been sent to my support, as soon as all my reserves were engaged I ordered him forward, and about one-half of his command assisted in taking possession of this commanding position. While looking for a point at which to post the batteries I had sent for, I was wounded. At that time my troops were in the finest spirits. Some of the commanding officers of the regiment were riding up and down in front of their men with the colors captured from the enemy in their hands; the cheers almost rent the skies with their cheers; there was the greatest good feeling that I have ever witnessed on the field of battle.

In his official report Hooker says:

> The whole morning had been one of unusual animation to me and fraught with the grandest events. The conduct of my troops was sublime, and the occasion almost lifted me to the skies, and its memories will ever remain with me. My command followed the fugitives closely until we had passed the cornfield a quarter of a mile or more, when I was removed from my saddle in the act of falling out of it from loss of blood, having been previously struck without my knowledge.

Although Hooker had been open and unsparing, vehement even, in his criticism and denunciation of McClellan, that officer seems not to have stored it up against him. He had given him charge of the attack on Lee's left, and after the battle recommended his promotion to the rank of brigadier-general in the regular army and wrote him the following kindly and appreciative letter:

Grave of Private John Marshall, Company L, 28th Pennsylvania. Photo taken looking almost west in the open field south of the Smoketown Road. *Library of Congress.*

HEADQUARTERS ARMY OF THE POTOMAC,
Sharpsburg, September 20, 1862.

Maj. Gen. JOSEPH HOOKER,
Commanding Corps:

MY DEAR HOOKER: I have been very sick the last few days, and just able to go where my presence was absolutely necessary, so I could not come to see you and thank you for what you did the other day, and express my intense regret and sympathy for your unfortunate wound. Had you not been wounded when you were, I believe the result of the battle would have been the entire destruction of the rebel army, for I know that, with you at its head, your corps would have kept on until it gained the main road. As a slight expression of what I think you merit, I have requested that the brigadier-general's commission rendered vacant by Mansfield's death may be given to you. I will this evening write a private note to the President on the subject, and I am glad to assure you that, so far as I can learn, it is the universal feeling of the army that you are the most deserving in it. With the sincere hope that your health may soon be restored, so that you may again be with us in the field, I am, my dear general, your sincere friend,

GEO. B. MCCLELLAN,
Major- General.[10]

As Hooker was borne to the rear Sumner's Second Corps was met. Sumner says that it was some distance to the rear where he passed Hooker, but that he saw nothing of his corps at all, as he was advancing with his command on the field, that it had been dispersed and routed, there was no question about that. He sent one of his staff officers to find where it was, and General Ricketts, the only officer he could find, said he could not raise 300 men of the corps. Had General Ricketts confined the information given to the condition of his own division, he would have been nearer the truth. Hartsuff's Brigade had been roughly handled by the enemy. Duryée and Christian had been feebly handled by their brigade commanders and almost entirely neglected when they were withdrawn from the front, and the division commander seems to have lacked the disposition or energy to gather his regiments, which was in the woods and fields in the rear. The

---

[10] Pasted by Carman into the manuscript. U. S. War Department, *War of the Rebellion: A Compilation of the Official Records of the Union and Confederate Armies* (hereafter cited as *O.R.*), Series I, vol. 19, part I, p. 219.

A dead Confederate soldier and the grave of Lt. John A. Clark of the 7th Michigan. This view is looking west along the torn down fence and initial position of Lawton's (Douglass) Brigade. *Library of Congress.*

division carried 3,158 officers and men into action, and lost 1,204 killed, wounded and missing; of the more than 1,900 remaining, less than 200 could be collected by noon, on the morning of the 18th but 1,008 were reported, showing a loss by straggling of 946. Meade's Division was in better shape. Out of the less than 3,000 carried into action, it had sustained a loss of 573 killed, wounded, and missing; it was not demoralized or routed, true it is that the brigades had been dislocated, but these had preserved their organization, three of Seymour's were in the S. Poffenberger woods and had rallied and moved forward to the support of Crawford's men in the East Woods; Magilton's Brigade had been badly punished, but had rallied in the North Woods, and there also, was Anderson's Brigade, in good shape and upon which Sumner rallied a part of Sedgwick's Division when driven from the West Woods, an hour later. The reason Sumner did not see these men was because they were to the right of his line of march. Of Doubleday's Division, Gibbon's Brigade had lost heavily, but the staunch "Iron Brigade" was united in the North Woods, and Phelps' was near it. Hofmann's Brigade was intact and had not been engaged, and Patrick was still in the fight and, with Goodrich's small brigade of the Twelfth Corps, holding an advanced position in the West Woods, and confronting Early. The greater part of two divisions were where they had started from in the morning, had suffered loss but were not dispersed or routed. There was fight in them yet and they would have proven it had they been called upon.

Of the Twelfth Corps Sumner says: "There were some troops lying down on the left which I took to be Mansfield's command. In the meantime General Mansfield had been killed, and a portion of his corps had been thrown into confusion." Palfrey says: "At somewhere about 9 o'clock, the Twelfth Corps seems to have about lost all aggressive force." Neither of these gallant soldiers would willingly make a misstatement and what yet they here say is far from the truth. Of Williams' Division four regiments of Crawford's Brigade had done some credible fighting and accomplished results; they had suffered loss, and were in and about the north part of the East Woods, two regiments of this brigade, the 124th and 125th Pennsylvania, were in the open ground south of the corn and opposite the Dunker Church, and on their right were the Purnell Legion of Goodrich's Brigade and the three old and tried regiments of Gordon's Brigade, much reduced in number, but not a bit wanting in aggression. The 107th New York of Gordon's Brigade was in second line in the East Woods, and the 13th New Jersey was approaching them; these two regiments, with the 125th Pennsylvania and seven companies of the 124th, had not been engaged, and their subsequent action showed that they had aggressive force. Greene's Division, on the left, had done some brilliant work and was to do more of it. In fact the entire Twelfth Corps, then about 6,000 strong, was

Brigadier General Joseph K. F. Mansfield.
Library of Congress.

preparing for an advance, and soon would have advanced had not Hooker been wounded and the approach of Sumner's Corps announced. It was high time; had it come two hours earlier and gone into action with the Twelfth Corps, Lee's left would have been crushed; had it come an hour earlier and closely followed the advantage won by the splendid fighting of the Twelfth Corps, the West Woods would have been in its possession before McLaws reached them; had it been on the field when the battle opened in the morning the day would have been won before noon.

Williams' Division became engaged at 7:30 a.m. and Greene's at about 8:15 a.m. Hood's Division fell back as the First Division was deploying, and by the united action of the two divisions Ripley's, Colquitt's and Garland's brigades were driven from the field before 8:45 a.m.

Note to Chapter 16

There has been much discussion, showing a wide divergence of opinion, as to where General Mansfield was mortally wounded. At least seven places have been indicated on the field where it occurred. Colonel Rogers, 31st [21st] New York, Patrick's Brigade, states that he saw him killed, beyond D. R. Miller's barn, in the West Woods. As Mansfield never crossed the Hagerstown road, Rogers is in error, probably mistaking Col. Goodrich for Mansfield. Another statement is that he was shot in D. R. Miller's orchard, but he was not on that part of the field after he had led his corps forward. Two places have been indicated which, at the time, were 350 yards inside the Confederate lines. General Gordon reports that he was wounded "while making a bold reconnaissance of the woods through which we had just dashed." If Gordon refers to the North Woods, through which his own brigade advanced, he is in error; if he refers to the East Woods, through which a part of Crawford's Brigade deployed, he is nearer the fact. Colonel Jacob Higgins, 125th Pennsylvania, whose regiment was in line fronting the East Woods and north of the Smoketown road, reports that some of his men carried the general "off the field on their muskets until a blanket was procured" and these men say that where they saw him wounded was at a point in front of and to the left of the 128th Pennsylvania, in the edge of the East Woods, and about 120 yards west of the Smoketown road. Major John M. Gould says he was wounded about 35 yards east of the Smoketown road, and in his "History of the 10th Maine" gives a circumstantial account of the event. Gould, at the time, was adjutant of the 10th Maine. He says:

> The Confederate force in our front showed no colors. They appeared to be somewhat detached from and in advance of the main rebel line, and were about where the left of General Duryée's brigade might be

The Joseph K. F. Mansfield monument on the battlefield.
Author's collection.

supposed to have retreated. To General Mansfield we appeared to be firing into Duryée's troops; therefore he beckoned to me to cease the firing, and as this was the very last thing we proposed to do, the few who saw him did not understand what his motions meant, and so no attention was paid to him. He now rode down the hill from the 128th Pennsylvania, and passing quickly through H, A, K, E, I, G, and D (of the 10th Maine), ordering them to cease firing, he halted in front of C, at the earnest remonstrances of Captain Jordan and Sergeant Barnham, who asked him to see the gray coats of the enemy, and pointed out particular men of them who were then aiming their rifles at us and at him. The general was convinced, and remarked 'Yes, yes, you are right,' and was almost instantly hit. He turned and attempted to put his horse over the rails, but the animal had also been severely wounded and could not go over. Thereupon the general dismounted, and a gust of wind blowing open his coat we saw that he was wounded in the body. Sergeant Joe Merritt, Storer Knight, and I took the general to the rear, assisted for a while by a negro cook from Hooker's corps. We put the general into an ambulance in the woods in front of which we had deployed, and noticed that General Gordon was just at that moment posting the 107th New York in their front edge.

Appendix[11]

Order of Battle

Union

Army of the Potomac 55,956[12]
Major General George B. McClellan

General Headquarters

Escort
Independent Company Oneida (New York) Cavalry
4th United States Cavalry, Companies A and E

Provost Guard
Major William F. Hood
2nd United States Cavalry, Companies E, F, H, and K
8th United States, Companies A, D, F, and G
19th United States, Companies G and H

Headquarters Guard
93rd New York

---

[11] Carman published an order of battle and unit strength calculations as separate appendices. However, since I have modified it slightly to include only those units engaged in battle or on the field by September 17th, this chapter is not as Carman published it, but a new representation.

[12] Unit strengths listed as Carman presented them in his manuscript and appendixes with little clarification except using the *Official Records* to separate the strengths of attached artillery batteries from their infantry brigades where necessary. Carman calculated engaged strengths and not present for duty. Still, he's just as likely to be as accurate as other sources.

First Army Corps 9,438
Major General Joseph Hooker

1st Division 3,425
Brigadier General Abner Doubleday

1st Brigade 425
Colonel Walter
Phelps Jr.
22nd New York
24th New York
30th New York
84th New York*
2nd United States
Sharpshooters
*Also known as the
14th Brooklyn

2nd Brigade 750
Lt. Colonel J.
William Hofmann
7th Indiana
76th New York
95th New York
56th Pennsylvania

3rd Brigade 829
Brigadier General
Marsena R. Patrick
21st New York
23rd New York
35th New York
80th New York

4th Brigade 971
Brigadier General John Gibbon
19th Indiana
2nd Wisconsin
6th Wisconsin
7th Wisconsin

Artillery 450
1st New Hampshire Battery
Battery D, 1st Rhode Island
Battery L, 1st New York
Battery B, 4th United States

2d Division 3,158
Brigadier General James B. Ricketts

1st Brigade 1,100
Brigadier General
Abram Duryée
97th New York
104th New York
105th New York
107th Pennsylvania

2nd Brigade 937
Colonel William A.
Christian
26th New York
94th New York
88th Pennsylvania
90th Pennsylvania

3rd Brigade 1,000
Brigadier General
George L. Hartsuff
12th Massachusetts
13th Massachusetts
83rd New York
11th Pennsylvania

Artillery 121
Battery F, 1st Pennsylvania
Battery C, Pennsylvania Light

3rd Division 2,855
Brigadier General George G. Meade

1st Brigade
Brigadier General Truman Seymour
1st Pennsylvania Reserves
2nd Pennsylvania Reserves
5th Pennsylvania Reserves
6th Pennsylvania Reserves
13th Pennsylvania Reserves

2nd Brigade
Colonel Albert L. Magilton
3rd Pennsylvania Reserves
4th Pennsylvania Reserves
7th Pennsylvania Reserves
8th Pennsylvania Reserves

3rd Brigade
Lt. Colonel Robert Anderson
9th Pennsylvania Reserves
10th Pennsylvania Reserves
11th Pennsylvania Reserves
12th Pennsylvania Reserves

Artillery 248
Battery A, 1st Pennsylvania Light
Battery B, 1st Pennsylvania Light
Battery C, 5th United States

Second Army Corps 16,065
Major General Edwin V. Sumner

1st Division 4,275
Major General Israel B. Richardson

1st Brigade 1,339
Brigadier General John
C. Caldwell
5th New Hampshire
7th New York
61st & 64th New York
81st Pennsylvania

2nd Brigade 1,340
Brigadier General
Thomas F. Meagher
29th Massachusetts
63rd New York
69th New York
88th New York

3rd Brigade 1,336
Colonel John R.
Brooke
2nd Delaware
52nd New York
57th New York
66th New York
53rd Pennsylvania

Artillery 246
Battery B, 1st New York
Batteries A & C, 4th United States

2nd Division 5,681
Major General John Sedgwick

1st Brigade 1,691
Brigadier General
Willis A. Gorman
15th Massachusetts
1st Minnesota
34th New York
82nd New York
Massachusetts
Sharpshooters, 1st
Company
Minnesota
Sharpshooters, 2nd
Company

2nd Brigade 1,800
Brigadier General
Oliver O. Howard
69th Pennsylvania
71st Pennsylvania
72nd Pennsylvania
106th Pennsylvania

3rd Brigade 1,946
Brigadier General
Napoleon J. T. Dana
19th Massachusetts
20th Massachusetts
7th Michigan
42nd New York
59th New York

Artillery 244
Battery A, 1st Rhode Island
Battery I, 1st United States

3rd Division 5,740
Brigadier General William H. French

1st Brigade 1,751
Brigadier General
Nathan Kimball
14th Indiana
8th Ohio
132nd Pennsylvania
7th West Virginia

2nd Brigade 2,191
Colonel Dwight
Morris
14th Connecticut
108th New York
130th Pennsylvania

3rd Brigade 1,798
Brigadier General
Max Weber
1st Delaware
5th Maryland
4th New York

Unattached Artillery 369
Battery G, 1st New York
Battery B, 1st Rhode Island
Battery G, 1st Rhode Island

Fifth Army Corps 12,930[13]
Major General Fitz John Porter

1st Division
Major General George W. Morell

1st Brigade	2nd Brigade	3rd Brigade
Colonel James Barnes	Brigadier General Charles Griffin	Colonel Thomas B. W. Stockton
2nd Maine	2nd District of Columbia	20th Maine
18th Massachusetts	9th Massachusetts	16th Michigan
22nd Massachusetts	32nd Massachusetts	12th New York
1st Michigan	4th Michigan	17th New York
13th New York	14th New York	44th New York
25th New York	62nd Pennsylvania	83rd Pennsylvania
118th Pennsylvania		Michigan Sharpshooters, Brady's Company
Massachusetts Sharpshooters, 2nd Company		

Unassigned
1st United States Sharpshooters

Artillery
Battery C, Massachusetts Light
Battery C, 1st Rhode Island
Battery D, 5th United States

2nd Division
Brigadier General George Sykes

1st Brigade	2nd Brigade
Lt. Colonel Robert C. Buchanan	Major Charles S. Lovell
3rd United States	1st & 6th United States
4th United States	2nd & 10th United States
12th United States, 1st Battalion	11th United States
12th United States, 2nd Battalion	17th United States
14th United States, 1st Battalion	
14th United States, 2nd Battalion	

---

[13] *O.R.*, Series I, vol. 19, part I, p. 67.

<u>3rd Brigade</u>
Colonel Gouverneur K. Warren
5th New York
10th New York

<u>Artillery</u>
Batteries E & G, 1st United States
Battery I, 5th United States
Battery K, 5th United States

<u>Artillery Reserve</u> 950
Battery A, 1st Battalion New York
Battery B, 1st Battalion New York
Battery C, 1st Battalion New York
Battery D, 1st Battalion New York
5th New York Battery
Battery K, 1st United States
Battery G, 4th United States

Sixth Army Corps 12,300[14]
Major General William B. Franklin

1st Division
Major General Henry W. Slocum

<u>1st Brigade</u>
Colonel Alfred T.
A. Torbert
1st New Jersey
2nd New Jersey
3rd New Jersey
4th New Jersey

<u>2nd Brigade</u>
Colonel Joseph J. Bartlett
5th Maine
16th New York
27th New York
96th Pennsylvania

<u>3rd Brigade</u>
Brigadier General
John Newton
18th New York
31st New York
32nd New York
95th Pennsylvania

<u>Artillery</u>
Battery A, Maryland Light
Battery A, Massachusetts Light
Battery A, New Jersey Light
Battery D, 2nd United States

[14] *O.R.*, Series I, vol. 19, part I, p. 67.

2nd Division
Major General William F. Smith

1st Brigade	2nd Brigade	3rd Brigade 1,684
Brigadier General	Brigadier General	Colonel William H.
Winfield S. Hancock	William T. H. Brooks	Irwin
6th Maine	2nd Vermont	7th Maine
43rd New York	3rd Vermont	20th New York
49th Pennsylvania	4th Vermont	33rd New York
137th Pennsylvania	5th Vermont	49th New York
5th Wisconsin	6th Vermont	77th New York

Artillery
Battery B, Maryland Light
1st New York Light Battery
Battery F, 5th United States

Ninth Army Corps 12,765
Major General Ambrose E. Burnside
Brigadier General Jacob D. Cox

1st Division 3,248
Brigadier General Orlando B. Willcox

1st Brigade 1,395	2nd Brigade 1,623	Artillery 246
Colonel Benjamin C.	Colonel Thomas	8th Battery Massachusetts
Christ	Welsh	Light
28th Massachusetts	8th Michigan	Battery E, 2nd United
17th Michigan	46th New York	States
79th New York	45th Pennsylvania	
50th Pennsylvania	100th Pennsylvania	

2nd Division 3,254
Brigadier General Samuel D. Sturgis

1st Brigade 1,412	2nd Brigade 1,601	Artillery 241
Brigadier General	Brigadier General	Battery D, Pennsylvania
James Nagle	Edward Ferrero	Light
2nd Maryland	21st Massachusetts	Battery E, 4th United
6th New Hampshire	35th Massachusetts	States
9th New Hampshire	51st New York	
48th Pennsylvania	51st Pennsylvania	

3rd Division 2,914
Brigadier General Isaac P. Rodman

<u>1st Brigade</u> 943
Colonel Harrison S.
Fairchild
9th New York
89th New York
103rd New York
Co. K, 9th New York
Infantry (Battery)

<u>2nd Brigade</u> 1,848
Colonel Edward
Harland
8th Connecticut
11th Connecticut
16th Connecticut

4th Rhode Island

<u>Artillery</u> 123
Battery A, 5th United
States

Kanawha Division 3,154
Colonel Eliakim P. Scammon

<u>1st Brigade</u> 1,026
Colonel Hugh B. Ewing
12th Ohio
23rd Ohio
30th Ohio
Gilmore's Company West Virginia
Cavalry
Harrison's Company West Virginia
Cavalry
1st Battery Ohio Light Artillery

<u>2nd Brigade</u> 2,128
Colonel George Crook
11th Ohio
28th Ohio
36th Ohio
Schambeck's Company Chicago
Dragoons

Kentucky Light Artillery

<u>Unattached</u>
6th New York Cavalry
Ohio Cavalry, 3d Independent Co.

<u>Unattached Artillery</u> 195[15]
Batteries L & M 3rd United States
Battery L, 2nd New York

---

[15] Clemens, 582.

Twelfth Army Corps 7,631
Brigadier General Joseph K. Mansfield

1st Division 4,735
Brigadier General Alpheus S. Williams

1st Brigade 2,525
Brigadier General
Samuel W. Crawford
10th Maine
28th New York
46th Pennsylvania
124th Pennsylvania
125th Pennsylvania
128th Pennsylvania

3rd Brigade 2,210
Brigadier General George H.
Gordon
27th Indiana
2nd Massachusetts
13th New Jersey
107th New York
3rd Wisconsin

2nd Division 2,504
Brigadier General George S. Greene

1st Brigade 1,191
Lt. Colonel Hector
Tyndale
5th Ohio
7th Ohio
66th Ohio
28th Pennsylvania

2nd Brigade 536
Colonel Henry J.
Stainrook
3rd Maryland
102nd New York
111th Pennsylvania

3rd Brigade 777
Colonel William B.
Goodrich
3rd Delaware
Purnell Legion
60th New York
78th New York

Artillery Battalion 392
4th Maine Battery
6th Maine Battery
Battery M, 1st New York
10th New York Battery
Battery E, Pennsylvania Light
Battery F, Pennsylvania Light
Battery F, 4th United States

Cavalry Division 4,320
Brigadier General Alfred Pleasonton

<u>1st Brigade</u>
Major Charles J. Whiting
5th United States Cavalry
6th United States Cavalry

<u>2nd Brigade</u>
Colonel John F. Farnsworth
8th Illinois Cavalry
3rd Indiana Cavalry
1st Massachusetts Cavalry
8th Pennsylvania Cavalry

<u>3rd Brigade</u>
Colonel Richard H. Rush
4th Pennsylvania Cavalry
6th Pennsylvania Cavalry

<u>4th Brigade</u>
Colonel Andrew T. McReynolds
1st New York Cavalry
12th Pennsylvania Cavalry

<u>5th Brigade</u>
Colonel Benjamin F. Davis
8th New York Cavalry
3rd Pennsylvania Cavalry

<u>Artillery Battalion</u>
Battery A, 2nd United States
Batteries B & L, 2nd United States
Battery M, 2nd United States
Batteries C & G, 3rd United States

Army of Northern Virginia 37,351
General Robert E. Lee

Longstreet's Command 17,646
Major General James Longstreet

McLaw's Division 2,961
Major General Lafayette McLaws

<u>Kershaw's Brigade</u> 858	<u>Barksdale's Brigade</u> 858	<u>Semmes' Brigade</u> 709
Brigadier General	Brigadier General	Brigadier General
Joseph B. Kershaw	William Barksdale	Paul J. Semmes
2nd South Carolina	13th Mississippi	10th Georgia
3rd South Carolina	17th Mississippi	53rd Georgia
7th South Carolina	18th Mississippi	15th Virginia
8th South Carolina	21st Mississippi	32nd Virginia

<u>Cobb's Brigade</u> 398
Lt. Colonel Christopher C. Sanders
16th Georgia
24th Georgia
Cobb's Legion
15th North Carolina

<u>Cabell's Battalion</u>
Manly's North Carolina Battery
Pulaski Georgia Battery
Richmond Fayette Artillery
1st Richmond Howitzers
Troup Georgia Battery

Anderson's Division 4,000
Major General Richard H. Anderson

Wilcox's Brigade	Mahone's Brigade	Featherston's Brigade
Colonel Alfred Cumming	Colonel William A. Parham	Colonel Carnot Posey
8th Alabama	6th Virginia	12th Mississippi
9th Alabama	12th Virginia	16th Mississippi
10th Alabama	16th Virginia	19th Mississippi
11th Alabama	41st Virginia	2nd Mississippi Bn.

Armistead's Brigade	Pryor's Brigade	Wright's Brigade
Brigadier General Lewis A. Armistead	Brigadier General Roger A. Pryor	Brigadier General Ambrose R. Wright
9th Virginia	14th Alabama	44th Alabama
14th Virginia	2nd Florida	3rd Georgia
38th Virginia	5th Florida	22nd Georgia
53rd Virginia	8th Florida	48th Georgia
57th Virginia	3rd Virginia	

Saunders' Battalion
Donaldsonville Louisiana Battery
Norfolk Virginia Battery
Lynchburg Virginia Battery
Grimes's Virginia Battery

Jones' Division 1,540
Brigadier General David R. Jones

Garnett's Brigade 261	Jenkins' Brigade 755	Kemper's Brigade 443
Brigadier General Richard B. Garnett	Colonel Joseph Walker	Brigadier General James L. Kemper
8th Virginia	1st South Carolina	1st Virginia
18th Virginia	2nd South Carolina	7th Virginia
19th Virginia	5th South Carolina	11th Virginia
28th Virginia	6th South Carolina	17th Virginia
56th Virginia	4th South Carolina Bn.	24th Virginia
	Palmetto Sharpshooters	

Artillery 81
Wise Virginia Battery

Toomb's Division (temporary)* 1,852
Brigadier General Robert Toombs

Toombs' Brigade 638	Drayton's Brigade 465	Anderson's Brigade 749
Colonel Henry	Brigadier General	Brigadier General
L. Benning	Thomas F. Drayton	George T. Anderson
2nd Georgia	50th Georgia	1st Georgia Regulars
15th Georgia	51st Georgia	7th Georgia
17th Georgia	15th South Carolina	8th Georgia
20th Georgia	3rd South Carolina Bn.	9th Georgia
	Phillip's Legion	11th Georgia

*This temporary division, split from D. R. Jones', was created at the onset of the campaign at Leesburg, Virginia.

Walker's Division
Brigadier General John G. Walker

Walker's Brigade 2,279	Ransom's Brigade 1,715
Colonel Van H. Manning	Brigadier General Robert Ransom Jr.
3rd Arkansas	24th North Carolina
27th North Carolina	25th North Carolina
46th North Carolina	35th North Carolina
48th North Carolina	49th North Carolina
30th Virginia	Branch's Virginia Battery
French's Virginia Battery	

Hood's Division 2,304
Brigadier General John B. Hood

Hood's Brigade 854	Law's Brigade 1,146
Colonel William T. Wofford	Colonel Evander M. Law
18th Georgia	4th Alabama
Hampton Legion	2nd Mississippi
1st Texas	11th Mississippi
4th Texas	6th North Carolina
5th Texas	

Artillery Battalion 304
German South Carolina Battery
Palmetto South Carolina Battery
Rowan North Carolina Battery

<u>Evans's Brigade</u> 399
Brigadier General Nathan G. Evans*
Colonel Peter. F. Stevens
17th South Carolina
18th South Carolina
22nd South Carolina
23rd South Carolina
Holcombe Legion
Macbeth South Carolina Battery

*Believed he was a division commander and had Col. Stevens command the brigade.

Corps Artillery

<u>Lee's Battalion</u> 318
Ashland Virginia Battery
Bedford Virginia Battery
Brook's South Carolina Battery
Eubanks' Virginia Battery
Madison Louisiana Battery
Parker's Virginia Battery

<u>Washington Artillery Bn.</u> 278
1st Company
2nd Company
3rd Company
4th Company

Jackson's Command 14,584
Major General Thomas J. Jackson

Ewell's Division 4,127
Brigadier General Alexander R. Lawton

<u>Lawton's Brigade</u> 1,250
Colonel Marcellus
Douglass
13th Georgia
26th Georgia
31st Georgia
38th Georgia
60th Georgia
61st Georgia

<u>Early's Brigade</u> 1,331
Brigadier General
Jubal A. Early
13th Virginia
25th Virginia
31st Virginia
44th Virginia
49th Virginia
52nd Virginia
58th Virginia

<u>Trimble's Brigade</u> 761
Colonel James
A. Walker
15th Alabama
12th Georgia
21st Georgia
21st North Carolina

Hay's Brigade 598
Brigadier General Harry T. Hays
5th Louisiana
6th Louisiana
7th Louisiana
8th Louisiana
14th Louisiana

Artillery 223
Johnson's Virginia Battery
Louisiana Guard Artillery
First Maryland Battery
Staunton Virginia Battery

A. P. Hill's Light Division 2,568*
Major General Ambrose P. Hill

Branch's Brigade
Brigadier General
Lawrence O. Branch
7th North Carolina
18th North Carolina
28th North Carolina
33rd North Carolina
37th North Carolina

Gregg's Brigade
Brigadier General
Maxcy Gregg
1st South Carolina Prov. Army
1st South Carolina Rifles
12th South Carolina
13th South Carolina
14th South Carolina

Field's Brigade
Colonel John M.
Brockenbrough
40th Virginia
47th Virginia
55th Virginia
22nd Virginia Bn.

Archer's Brigade
Brigadier General James
J. Archer
5th Alabama Battalion
19th Georgia
1st Tennessee Provisional Army
7th Tennessee
14th Tennessee

Pender's Brigade
Brigadier General William
D. Pender
16th North Carolina
22nd North Carolina
34th North Carolina
38th North Carolina

Artillery Battalion 337
Crenshaw's Virginia Battery
Fredericksburg Virginia Battery
Pee Dee South Carolina Battery
Purcell Virginia Battery

*Does not include Field's or Pender's Brigades, as they were not actively engaged.

Jones' Division 2,094
Brigadier General John R. Jones

Stonewall Brigade 489
Colonel Andrew
J. Grigsby
4th Virginia
5th Virginia
27th Virginia
33rd Virginia

Taliaferro's Brigade 543
Colonel James
W. Jackson
47th Alabama
48th Alabama
23rd Virginia
37th Virginia

Jones' Brigade
Cpt. John E. Penn
21st Virginia
42nd Virginia
48th Virginia
1st Virginia Bn.

Starke's Brigade 706
Brigadier General
William E. Starke
1st Louisiana
2nd Louisiana
9th Louisiana
10th Louisiana
15th Louisiana
Coppens' Battalion

Andrew's Battalion 310
Alleghany Virginia Battery
Brockenbrough's Maryland Battery
Danville Virginia Battery
Lee Virginia Battery
Rockbridge Virginia Battery

D. H. Hill's Division 5,795
Major General Daniel H. Hill

Ripley's Brigade 1,349
Brigadier General
Roswell S. Ripley
4th Georgia
44th Georgia
1st North Carolina
3rd North Carolina

Garland's Brigade 756
Colonel Duncan
K. McRae
5th North Carolina
12th North Carolina
13th North Carolina
20th North Carolina
23rd North Carolina

Anderson's Brigade
1,174
Brigadier General
George B. Anderson
2nd North Carolina
4th North Carolina
14th North Carolina
30th North Carolina

Rodes' Brigade 850
Brigadier General Robert E. Rodes
3rd Alabama
5th Alabama
6th Alabama
12th Alabama
26th Alabama

Colquitt's Brigade 1,320
Colonel Alfred H. Colquitt
13th Alabama
6th Georgia
23rd Georgia
27th Georgia
28th Georgia

Artillery Battalion 346
Hardaway's Alabama Battery
Jefferson Davis Alabama Battery
Jones' Virginia Battery
King William Virginia Battery

Artillery Reserve 621
Brigadier General William N. Pendleton

Cutts's Artillery Battalion 319[16]
Blackshear's Georgia Battery
Irwin's Georgia Battery
Patterson's Georgia Battery
Ross' Georgia Battery

Jones' Artillery Battalion 302[17]
Morris Virginia Battery
Orange Virginia Battery
Turner's Virginia Battery
Wimbish's Virginia Battery

Miscellaneous Artillery
Cutshaw's Virginia Battery
Dixie Virginia Battery
Magruder Virginia Battery
Rice's Virginia Battery

Cavalry 4,500
Major General J .E. B. Stuart

Hampton's Brigade
Brigadier General Wade Hampton
1st North Carolina Cavalry
2nd South Carolina Cavalry
Cobb's Georgia Legion
Jeff Davis Legion

Robertson's Brigade
Colonel Thomas T. Munford
2nd Virginia Cavalry
7th Virginia Cavalry
12th Virginia Cavalry

Fitz-Hugh Lee's Brigade
Brigadier General Fitz-Hugh Lee
1st Virginia Cavalry
3rd Virginia Cavalry
4th Virginia Cavalry
5th Virginia Cavalry
9th Virginia Cavalry

Horse Artillery
Chew's Virginia Battery
Hart's South Carolina Battery
Pelham's Virginia Battery

---

[16] Clemens, 599.
[17] Ibid.

Bibliography

Carman, Ezra A. *The Maryland Campaign of September 1862: Vol. II: Antietam.* Edited by Thomas G. Clemens. El Dorado Hills: Savas Beatie LLC, 2012.

Carman, Ezra A. and Emmor B. Cope. "Atlas of the Battlefield of Antietam, prepared under the direction of the Antietam Battlefield Board, Lieut. Col. Geo. W. Davis, U.S.A., president, Gen. E.A. Carman, U.S.V., Gen. H Heth, C.S.A. Surveyed by Lieut. Col. E.B. Cope, engineer, H.W. Mattern, assistant engineer, of the Gettysburg National Park. Drawn by Charles H. Ourand, 1899. Position of troops by Gen. E. A. Carman. Published by authority of the Secretary of War, under the direction of the Chief of Engineers, U.S. Army, 1908.", 1904, Revised Edition 1908, Library of Congress.

Frassanito, William A. *Antietam: The Photographic Legacy of America's Bloodiest Day.* Gettysburg: Thomas Publications, 1978.

Gottfried, Bradley M. *The Maps of Antietam: An Atlas of the Antietam (Sharpsburg) Campaign, Including the Battle of South Mountain, September 2-20, 1862.* El Dorado Hills: Savas Beatie LLC, 2012.

Johnson, Curt and Richard C. Anderson Jr. *Artillery Hell: The Employment of Artillery at Antietam.* College Station: Texas A&M University Press, 1995.

Pierro, Joseph, ed. *The Maryland Campaign of September 1862: Ezra A. Carman's Definitive Study of the Union and Confederate Armies at Antietam.* New York: Taylor & Francis Group, LLC, 2008.

Rawle, William Brooke. *History of the Third Pennsylvania Cavalry, Sixtieth Regiment Pennsylvania Volunteers, in the American Civil War 1861-1865.* Philadelphia: Franklin Printing Company, 1905.

Sid Meier's Antietam!. Firaxis Games, 1999.

Thomson, O. R. Howard and William H. Rauch. *History of the "Bucktails" Kane Rifle Regiment of the Pennsylvania Reserve Corps (13th Pennsylvania Reserves, 42nd of the Line).* Philadelphia: Electric Printing Company, 1906.

U. S. War Department. *The War of the Rebellion: A Compilation of the Official Records of the Union and Confederate Armies.* 128 vols. Washington D. C.: Government Printing Office, 1880-1901.

Index

211

Ezra A. Carman was born in 1839 and served as colonel of the 13th New Jersey Infantry regiment from 1862 to 1864, moving on to brigade command during Sherman's March to the Sea. After the war, he served as chief clerk of the United States Department of Agriculture, historical expert for the Antietam National Battlefield, and Chairman of the Chickamauga-Chattanooga National Battlefield Commission. He passed away in 1909.

Brad Butkovich has a Bachelor of Arts degree in history from Georgia Southern University. He has published several books on the American Civil War including studies on the Battle of Pickett's Mill and Allatoona Pass. He has always had a keen interest in Civil War history, photography and cartography, all of which have come together in his current projects.

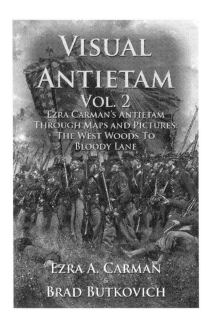

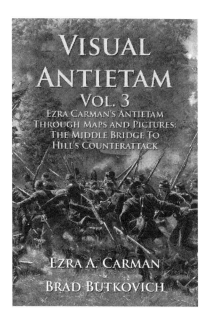

1st Quarter 2019

2nd Quarter 2019

Made in the USA
Columbia, SC
18 January 2022

54267730R00126